William McKinley

McKinley's masterpieces

Selections from the public addresses in and out of Congress of William McKinley

William McKinley

McKinley's masterpieces
Selections from the public addresses in and out of Congress of William McKinley

ISBN/EAN: 9783337234140

Printed in Europe, USA, Canada, Australia, Japan

Cover: Foto ©Suzi / pixelio.de

More available books at **www.hansebooks.com**

McKINLEY'S MASTERPIECES

SELECTIONS

FROM THE PUBLIC ADDRESSES IN AND OUT OF CONGRESS

OF

WILLIAM McKINLEY

Colonial Press:

C. H. Simonds & Co., Boston, Mass., U. S. A.

Electrotyped by Geo. C. Scott & Sons

INTRODUCTORY STATEMENT.

WILLIAM McKINLEY stands high among America's greatest orators. This is the estimate of his own time, and it will be not less the verdict of impartial history. Although his speeches have been many, in the halls of Congress, in political campaigns, and upon the thousand and one occasions where oratorical genius is demanded, there is no sameness, no monotony, no dullness in the utterances of McKinley. For clearness of statement, irrefutable logic, vigor of expression, lofty moral tone, and those qualities which carry conviction, he has had few equals and no superiors. To read his speeches is to take lessons in the intricate problems of American political life, and to gain a true perception of the deeper philosophy underlying wise and salutary popular government.

No American of this age can afford not to read McKinley's speeches. To meet the needs of the busy man, this selection of the masterpieces of McKinley's thought and diction has been prepared. And its compiler feels assured that no one will read even these few pages without gaining a higher ideal of public duty and a stronger love of country.

CONTENTS

INTRODUCTORY STATEMENT VII

BIOGRAPHICAL SKETCH . . . XI

I. THE REPUBLICAN PARTY . 21
    I. BRIEF AND TO THE POINT.
    II. BEFORE THE MICHIGAN CLUB

II THE PROTECTIVE TARIFF . . 29
    I NUGGETS.
    II ON THE MILLS BILL.
    III. THE GORMAN TARIFF
    IV THE TARIFF COMMISSION
    V WHAT PROTECTION MEANS TO VIR
        GINIA.
    VI. THE MCKINLEY TARIFF OF 1896.

III. THE PURITY OF THE BALLOT So
    I. THE WAR IS OVER
    II. THE BLACK COLOR BEARER.
    III. FAIR ELECTIONS.

IV. FINANCE . . . 95
    I. THE PURCHASE OF GOVERNMENT
        BONDS.
    II. THE SILVER BILL.

V. THE INTERESTS OF LABOR . 101
    I. MULTUM IN PARVO.
    II. THE AMERICAN WORKINGMAN.
    III. THE EIGHT-HOUR LAW.

VI. Educational Topics . 108

    I. In a Nutshell.
    II. Our Public Schools.
    III. History of Oberlin College.
    IV. Education and Citizenship.

VII. Religion 120

    I. To the Epworth League.
    II. An Auxiliary to Religion.

VIII. Miscellaneous Addresses 126

    I. Civil Service Reform.
    II. Notification Address to Presi
       dent Harrison.
    III. Not a Candidate.
    IV. Prosperity and Politics.
    V. Presidential Candidates.
    VI. On Counting a Quorum.

IX. Memorial Day and Patriotism 140

    I. Gems of Patriotic Expression.
    II. Memorial Day Address.
    III. The American Volunteer Soldier.

X. Eulogies 158

    I. James A. Garfield.
    II. Ulysses S. Grant.
    III. John A. Logan.
    IV. Abraham Lincoln.

XI. Occasional Addresses . . 190

    I. New England and the Future.
    II. July Fourth at Woodstock.
    III. Dedication of the Ohio Building
    IV. Business Man in Politics.

In the Directory published in 1877, nearly twenty years ago, appears this modest notice of one of the newly elected members of the 45th Congress :

WILLIAM McKINLEY, JR., of Canton, was born at Niles, Ohio, February 26th, 1844; enlisted in the United States Army in May, 1861, as a private soldier in the 23d Ohio Volunteer Infantry, and was mustered out as captain of the same regiment and Brevet-Major ; was Prosecuting Attorney of Stark County, Ohio, 1869 '71 ; and was elected to the 45th Congress as a Republican, receiving 16,489 votes against 13,185 votes for L. L. Sanborn, Democrat, and 2,441 votes for John R. Powell, Greenback candidate.

This is the simple story told nearly twenty years ago of a new member of that House of Representatives, and the date conveniently divides the career of William McKinley into two great periods. Up to that time the young man had made a gallant record as a soldier, since then he has made an even greater record as a statesman.

In ancestry McKinley is a mixture of the

XI

Covenanter and the Puritan. His ancestors came originally from the western part of Scotland. During the religious persecutions they, with hundreds of Covenanters, fled to Ireland. From that country the two brothers, James and William, came to America, about twenty-five years before the battle of Bunker Hill. James, then only a boy, settled in York, Pennsylvania, where he married, and his son David fought under Washington in the Revolution. This David McKinley was the great-grand-father of the eminent statesman toward whom the eyes of the nation are now turned. After the War of 1812 David McKinley moved to Columbia County, Ohio, where he founded the Buckeye branch of the McKinley family.

Major McKinley's mother, now living in vigorous old age, was an Allison, of English blood. She is a woman of remarkable intellectual powers and a finely developed moral nature. His father, who died at the age of eighty-four, was a highly respected citizen of Poland, the extreme southwestern township of the original Western Reserve.

William McKinley, Jr., enjoyed the advantages of a fair, although not extensive, education. His learning has been acquired in the university of the world, grappling with life's sterner problems, rather than in the cloistered halls of the academy. For a short time he attended the Allegheny College, but, between study and school - teaching, he had not advanced far when the conflict between the States broke out. In June, 1861, an effective orator, who had frequently told of the horrors of slavery, spoke one evening in front of the village tavern in the little town of Poland. He called upon the people to rise to put down the incipient rebellion, and to punish the traitors who had fired upon the Stars and Stripes. Among his listeners was young William McKinley, Jr., then only seventeen years old, who had for several terms been a country schoolteacher.

The patriotic spirit of this little Western Reserve town contributed one company to the 23d Ohio regiment of the Union army. By a singular coincidence this regiment contained several names destined to rank high in the annals of fame, but none higher than that of the youthful school - teacher, who, against his father's wishes, had decided to bear his humble part in the great task of saving the Union. Of this regiment William S. Rosecrans was a colonel; Stanley Matthews, afterwards Justice of the Supreme Court, was the second officer, and Rutherford B. Hayes, afterwards Governor of Ohio and President of the United States, eventually assumed its command.

McKinley enlisted as a private, became a

staff-officer under General Hayes, and for
gallantry at Antietam was advanced to the
the grade of Lieutenant by Governor Todd,
of Ohio, and was afterwards brevetted Major
by President Lincoln. It will thus be seen
that the gallant Ohioan's military title is no
idle compliment, but was honourably earned
in the stubborn field of war. To relate the
part which the brave young officer took in all
the battles in which he was engaged would be
a task beyond the limits of this sketch. Military records, in describing the battle of Ope-
quan, fought under Sheridan, near Winchester,
relate that early in the forenoon Captain Mc-
Kinley, aide-de-camp, brought a verbal order
to General Duval, commanding the second
division, to take a new position. On receiving the order, Duval inquired by what route
he should move the command. After Mc-
Kinley had suggested a route, Duval declared
that he would not budge without definite orders, to which the youthful captain replied:
" By command of General Crook, I order you
to move your command up this ravine to a
position on the right of the army." This
forceful insistence, that orders intrusted to
him should be carried out, has been a prom-
inent characteristic in McKinley's great career. Whether those commands have come
from a superior officer in the field, or in the

voice of American electors, his loyal obedience has been alike unflagging.

General Sheridan, in his Memoirs, tells of meeting McKinley on his ride to Winchester, " Twenty miles away." The acquaintance then formed ripened with the years, and is among Major McKinley's delightful recollections. At the age of twenty-two, McKinley's military career was over, and he again entered civil life in Ohio. He studied law in the office of Judge Glidden, and took a brief course at the Albany law school, gaining admittance to the bar in 1867. In the little town of Canton, then a place of 5,000 inhabitants, the young attorney put out his shingle. His career at the bar was short, but brilliant. Before long years of experience could bring to him the full fruition of the lawyer's aspirations, he was called to public life by a demand of duty no less emphatic than that which had enlisted him in the war. Including his service as district attorney, he was only nine years in the practice of his profession before he was elected to the National House of Representatives, and that was the time when the modest narrative at the opening of this sketch was penned.

During this period, in 1871, Major McKinley was married to Miss Ida Saxton. Their family life has been most sweet and ennobling.

Two little girls were born to them, who each
in turn passed away.   Since the birth of their
second daughter, in 1873, Mrs. McKinley has
never seen a well day, and that calamity, with
the bereavement that came to them in the loss
of their little ones, has again emphasized the
truth that honour and fame cannot make good
the loss of loved ones.   Owing to her afflic-
tion, Mrs. McKinley rarely goes out and does
not give large receptions, or, in general, attend
to those social requirements which high official
position is supposed to entail.   The mutual
devotion of the rugged statesman and his frail
companion is one of the most touching examples of love and fidelity which the country
affords.   With   tender   care   and   unselfish
solicitude Major McKinley guards his wife,
and never gives expression to the slightest
disappointment when a much cherished plan
has to be put aside by reason of her infirmities.

The twenty years of Major McKinley's
public life have been full of achievements too
well known to need description.   They are a
part of our country's history, which nothing
can efface.   In all the aspects of greatness as
a legislator McKinley has conspicuously ex-
celled.   As a participant in the congressional
debates, he has had, since the war period,
almost no equal ; in that judicious management of forces and planning of campaign

done in the committee-room, but so indispensable to the success of legislation, there has been but one McKinley. As a manager he is par excellence. Another of McKinley's remarkable traits of character is his untiring industry; no detail that is related, however remotely, to large results, ever escapes his attention. By no accident of fatuitous circumstance did he attain his great eminence in Congress, which led to his selection as chairman of the ways and means committee, and majority leader on the floor. Strict attention to duty, untiring study of all public questions, conscientious devotion to the interests of the people, and sterling patriotism were the elements that made his success in Congress.

To summarize his achievements would be no light task. In the popular mind his name is enshrined with the great and beneficent principle of protection. This estimate is just and deserved, but it does not tell the whole truth. While McKinley is the greatest living champion of the doctrine of protection, he is in no sense a man of one idea. He is a grand all-around exponent of the principles of the Republican party, and not of any school or section of that magnificent organization. McKinley is preeminent as a protectionist only because that doctrine is pre-

eminent among the tenets of Republicanism.
But, back of any specific doctrine, he stands
squarely and strongly for the underlying principle of National Unity, in distinction from
State Sovereignty, and for those corollaries in
the philosophy of government which depend
upon the inseparable union idea. To those
battle-scarred veterans who made possible and
enduring our national unity, he has always
been a friend, and has invariably favored a
generous pension policy, believing that the
most which a grateful republic could do would
be only tardy justice. On the vexed question
of finance, McKinley now, and at all times, has
typified Republicanism. He has always been
unflinchingly for sound money, and at the
same time has been friendly to silver, — a
great American product, — and has striven
to secure, through appropriate legislation, its
largest possible use, consistent with the safe
standards of Republican policy. Civil service
reform has found in him a warm friend, although he does not fail to recognize the fact
that, in a large number of posts, those in sympathy with the administration in power can
be more efficient workers than those who are
in opposition. For the rights of labor Mc-
Kinley has always been a zealous champion.
While in Congress he worked for the eight-
hour law, and was one of the strongest advo-

cates of the bill for the settlement, by arbitration, of controversies between interstate car-
riers and their employees.

Democratic trickery unexpectedly put an
end to the congressional career of Mr.
McKinley. That party, having secured possession of the Legislature of Ohio, so gerry-
mandered the State that from McKinley's
old district an angel from heaven could not
have been elected as a Republican. This
was in 1890 that, after a vigorous campaign
and a stubborn fight, McKinley laid down his
arms before the omnipotence of the gerry-
mander. But such methods did not long
avail to check a great career. In 1891 he
was nominated for Governor of Ohio. That
was a year of great Democratic victories, and
in the four doubtful States in which gubernatorial elections were held, in Ohio alone, and
under the leadership of McKinley, were the
Republicans successful. Flower was elected
Governor of New York, Boies of Iowa, and
Russell of Massachusetts. But even in a
tidal wave year the Napoleon of protection
was too much for the hosts of Democracy.

Of McKinley's administration as Governor,
too fresh in the public mind to permit more
than a brief reference, one commendation is
sufficiently striking to tell the story. After a
brilliant campaign in 1891 he was elected

Governor by about 20,000, while after the people tried him two years in that new relation, his majority, after a spirited contest, was over 80,000. As chief executive of the great Commonwealth McKinley has shown a genius for administration quite as remarkable as he had previously shown in Congress as a legislator, or as a youth he had shown on the field of battle. Soldier, statesman, executive, man and orator of preeminent ability, rare integrity, genial and gentle manners, McKinley is an ideal of American citizenship, and one whose life is worthy of the closest study of all his fellow countrymen.

McKINLEY'S MASTERPIECES.

CHAPTER I.

THE REPUBLICAN PARTY.

IT IS fitting that these selections should begin with quotations from the speeches of Major McKinley on the general topic — The Republican Party. To this great historic party he has given a life of devoted service; it, in turn, has honored him to the full measure of possibility.

I. Brief and to the Point.

" My fellow citizens, let us cherish the principles of our party and consecrate ourselves anew to their triumph. We have but to put our trust in the people; we have but to keep in close touch with the people; we have but to hearken to the voice of the people, as it comes to us from every quarter; we have but to paint on our banners the sentiment the people have everywhere expressed at every election during the last three years — 'Patriotism, Protection and Prosperity,' to win another most glorious and decisive Republican National victory." — *Marquette Club, Chicago, Feb. 12, 1896.*

" It is not our habit or our history as Republicans to haul down or lower our colors. We put them where they are. We mean to keep them there." — *Columbus, O., June 8, 1893.*

" The past of the Republican party is secure, its glory fills the world with wonder and admiration, and inspires mankind with new hopes and grander aspirations. The future is now our field ; let us look to it. It opens with glorious possibilities and invites the party of ideas to enter and possess it. Let us appeal to the highest judgment and reason of the people, and our appeal will not be in vain." *Dayton, O., Oct. 18, 1887.*

" The Republican party stands for a foreign policy dictated by and imbued with a spirit that is genuinely American ; for a policy that will revive the National traditions and restore the National spirit which carried us proudly through the earlier years of the century. It stands for such a policy with all foreign nations as will insure, both to us and them, justice, impartiality, fairness, good faith, dignity, and honor. It stands for the Monroe doctrine as Monroe himself proclaimed it, about which there is no division whatever among the American people. It stands now, as ever, for honest money and a chance to earn it by honest toil. It stands for a currency of gold, silver, and paper with which to measure our exchanges, that shall be as sound as the Government and as untarnished as its honor." — *Lincoln Banquet, Chicago, Feb. 12, 1896.*

"No one need be in any doubt about what the Republican party stands for. Its own history makes that too palpable and clear to admit of doubt. It stands for a reunited and recreated Nation, based upon free and honest elections in every township, county, city, district and State in this great American Union. It stands for the American fireside and the flag of the Nation. It stands for the American farm, the American factory, and the prosperity of all the American people. It stands for a reciprocity that reciprocates and which does not yield up to another country a single day's labor that belongs to the American workingman. It stands for international agreements, which get as much as they give, upon terms of mutual advantage. It stands for an exchange of our surplus home products for such foreign products as we consume but do not produce. It stands for the reciprocity of Blaine; for the reciprocity of Harrison; for the restoration and extension of the principle embodied in the reciprocity provision of the Republican tariff in 1890."—*Lincoln Banquet, Chicago, Feb. 12, 1896.*

"Much as the Republican party has done, it has great things yet to do. It will be a mighty force in the future as it has been a mighty force in the past. Its glories will continue to blaze on the heights, a beacon to the world, pointing to a higher destiny for mankind, and the upholding and uplifting of a Nation approved of God. It will not pause in its march and achievements until the Flag, the Flag of the Stars, shall be the unquestioned symbol of sovereignty at home and of American rights abroad; until American labor shall be securely shielded from the degrading competition of the Old World, and our entire citizenship from the vicious and criminal classes who are crowding our shores : never while the advocates of a debased dollar threaten the country with its financial heresies; and never until the free right to vote in every corner of the country shall be protected under the law, and by the law, and for the law; never until the American ballot-box shall be

held as sacred as the American home." —
*Niles, Ohio, Gubernatorial Campaign, Oct. 22,
1891.*

II. " The Republican Party. It offers its past as a guarantee for its future."

" *Mr. President, Gentlemen of the Michigan
Republican Club:*— It gives me sincere pleasure
to meet with you to-night. I have not met
with the Republicans of Michigan since the
great victory of 1894 — the great national
victory and I bring to you my congratulations upon the proud part you bore in that
great conflict resulting so triumphantly for
Republican principles, and, as I believe, for the
best interests of the whole country. I cannot
believe that our principles are less dear to us
in their triumph than they were in their
temporary defeat. I cannot believe that the
principles which won a most unprecedented
victory from ocean to ocean require now either
modification or abandonment. They are
dearer and closer to the American heart than
they have ever been in the past, and notwithstanding the magnificent victory of 1894, and
notwithstanding these great principles are
cherished in the hearts of the American
people, there is still a greater and more significant battle to be fought in the near future,

before we can realize those principles in administration and legislation.

"While, in the situation of the country, there is no cause for congratulation, this is not the time to employ terms of distrust or aggravation. Times are bad enough, and the voice of encouragement is more appropriate than that of alarm and exaggeration. The realities are quite ugly enough, and it is the duty of each of us, by word and act, in so far as it can be done, to improve the present condition. But above all, we must not disparage our government. We must uphold it, and uphold it at all times and under all circumstances, notwithstanding that we may not be able to support the measures and policies of the present administration. Home prosperity is the only key to an easy treasury and a high credit. The Republican party never lowered the flag or the credit of the Government, but has exalted both. I agree with the President, in his recent message, that a predicament confronts us. When I was here six years ago, reading from his message, it was a condition that confronted us, and that condition was an overflowing treasury, under Republican legislation. Now I come back to you, and it is a predicament that confronts the people of the United States, because of a deficiency created by the legislation of a Democratic Congress and administration.

"I am sure, however, that there is wisdom and patriotism ample enough in the country to relieve ourselves from this or any other predicament, and to place us once more at the head of the nations of the world in credit, production, and prosperity. The Republican party needs but to adhere faithfully to its principles — to the principles enunciated by its great national conventions, which guided the republic for a third of a century in safety and honor, which gave the country an adequate revenue, and, while doing that, labor received comfortable wages and steady employment, which guarded every American interest at home and abroad with zealous care — principles, the application of which made us a nation of homes, of independent, prosperous freemen, where all had a fair chance and an equal opportunity in the race of life. You do not have to guess what the Republican party will do. The whole world knows its purposes. It has embodied them in law, and executed them in administration. It has bravely met every emergency, and has ever measured up to every new duty. It is dedicated to the people; it stands for the United States. It practises what it preaches, and fearlessly enforces what it teaches. Its simple code is home and country. Its central idea is the well-being of the people, and all the people.   It has no aim which does not take into account the honor of the Government, and the material advancement and happiness of the American people. The Republican party is neither an apology nor a reminiscence. It is proud of its past, and it sees greater usefulness in the future." — *Michigan Club, Feb. 22, 1895.*

CHAPTER II.

THE PROTECTIVE TARIFF.

WITH the great principle of protection the name of McKinley will ever be associated. In no land and in no age has this great economic policy had an abler expounder than he. Wherever this beneficent principle finds complete adoption, and its wisdom becomes demonstrated, McKinley's part in bringing about that prosperity and well-being of the social order which will inevitably result can nowhere be forgotten. He is the great philosopher of protection. To select from his voluminous expositions of this policy has been no easy task, but perhaps as representative a set of quotations as could be gathered is here found. One selection is taken from his estimate of the Mills Bill, the great tariff measure of the first Cleveland administration; while another comes from his speech on the Gorman tariff, the product of the second Cleveland administration. Another masterpiece is McKinley's discussion of the project for a tariff commission. It is here presented in part. "What protection means to Virginia" is an exposition of the effect of this economic philosophy, as applied to a particular locality; while McKinley's speech in presenting the tariff bill of 1890 is perhaps his most formal analysis of the protection plan, and from this masterpiece very generous extracts are here reproduced.

I. Nuggets.

"The protective system must stand, or fall, as a whole. As Burke said of liberty: 'It is the clear right of all, or of none. It is only perfect when universal.' It must be a protective tariff for all interests requiring the encouragement of the Government, or it must be free trade or a revenue tariff and rest alike upon all classes and all portions of the country."—*Address at Atlanta, Ga., Aug. 21, 1888.*

"We are faithfully wedded to the great principle of protection by every tie of party fealty and affection, and it is dearer to us now than ever before. Not only is it dearer to us as Republicans, but it has more devoted supporters among the great masses of the American people, irrespective of party, than at any previous period in our National history. It is everywhere recognized and endorsed as the great, masterful, triumphant American principle — the key to our prosperity in business, the safest prop to the Treasury of the United States, and the bulwark of our national independence and financial honor. The question of the continuance or abandonment of our protective system has been the one great, overshadowing, vital question in American politics ever since Mr. Cleveland opened the contest in December, 1887, to which the lamented James G. Blaine made swift reply from across the sea, and it will

continue the issue until a truly American
policy, for the good of America, is firmly
established and perpetuated. The fight will
go on — and must go on — until the American
system is everywhere recognized, until all
nations come to understand and respect it as
distinctly, and all Americans come to honor
or love it as dearly, as they do the American
flag. God grant the day may soon come
when all partizan contention over it is forever
at an end." *Lincoln Banquet, Marquette Club,
Chicago, Feb. 12, 1896.*

"I believe that it is the duty of American
Congressmen to legislate for American citizens, and not for foreign manufacturers. Let
us take care of our own interests, and look to
the well-being of our own citizens first."—
Speech on Tariff of 1883.

"Hamilton and Madison, Jefferson and
Calhoun, Clay and Webster, and Adams and
Jackson always asserted and maintained the
constitutionality of protection. Is Cleveland
a better constitutional lawyer than Jefferson?
Is Vilas more learned than Madison? Wat-
terson more profound than Clay? Adlai
Stevenson a better expounder of the Constitution than Andrew Jackson? Are all of them
combined safer interpreters of that great

instrument than the Supreme Court of the
United States, which has never failed, when
called upon, to sustain the constitutionality of
a protective tariff. If it is in violation of any
constitution, it is not that of the United
States. It is a manifest violation of the Constitution of the Confederate States. Possibly,
that is what they mean."—*At Beatrice, Ne-
braska, August 2, 1892.*

" Home competition will always bring prices
to a fair and reasonable level, and prevent
extortion and robbery. Success, or even
apparent success, in any business or enterprise, will incite others to engage in like enterprises, and then follows healthful strife, the
life of business, which inevitably results in
cheapening the article produced."—*Speech in
Congress on Wool Tariff Bill, 1878.*

" With me, protection is a deep conviction,
not a theory. I believe in it, and thus warmly
advocate it, because enveloped in it are my
country's highest development and greatest
prosperity ; out of it come the greatest gains
to the people, the greatest comforts to the
masses, the widest encouragement for manly
aspirations, with the best and largest rewards
for honest efforts dignifying and elevating
our citizenship, upon which the safety, the

purity, and permanency of our political system depend."— *Fifty-first Congress, May 7,
1890.*

" Protection builds up ; a revenue tariff
tears down. Protection brings hope and courage to heart and home ; free trade drives
them from both. Free trade levels down ;
protection levels up." - *Convention of Republican College Clubs, Ann Arbor, Mich., May
17, 1892.*

" Our philosophy includes the grower of the
wool, the weaver of the fabric, the seamstress,
and the tailor. Tariff reformers have no
thought of these toilers. They can bear their
hard tasks in pinching poverty for the sake of
cheap coats, which prove by far the dearest
when measured by sweat and toil. The tariff reformers concern themselves only about
cheap coats and cheap shoes. We do not
overlook the comfort of those who make the
coats and make the shoes, and will provide
the wool and the cloth, the hides and the
leather." *In reply to Mr. Cleveland, Toledo,
Ohio, Feb. 12, 1891.*

" The farmer is best off with a home market. The farmer himself knows this, and no
amount of rhetoric can deceive him. The

fathers of the republic saw it and proclaimed it. We can only have a profitable home market by encouraging manufacturing industries. "Plant the forge by the farm," is the old doctrine, and it is as true now as it was when uttered." — *Speech on Morrison Tariff Bill, House of Representatives, April 30, 1884.*

II. On the Mills Bill.

"What is a protective tariff? It is a tariff upon foreign imports so adjusted as to secure the necessary revenue, and judiciously imposed upon those foreign products the like of which are produced at home or the like of which we are capable of producing at home. It imposes the duty upon the competing foreign product; it makes it bear the burden or duty, and, as far as possible, luxuries only excepted, permits the non-competing foreign product to come in free of duty. Articles of common use, comfort and necessity, which we cannot produce here, it sends to the people untaxed and free from custom-house exactions. Tea, coffee, spices, and drugs are such articles, and under our system are upon the free list. It says to our foreign competitor, if you want to bring your merchandise here, your farm products here, your coal and iron ore, your wool, your salt, your pottery, your glass, your cottons and woolens, and sell alongside of our producers in our markets, we will make your product bear a duty; in effect, pay for the privilege of doing it.

"Our kind of tariff makes the competing foreign article carry the burden, draw the load, supply the revenue; and in performing this essential office it encourages at the same time our own industries and protects our own people in their chosen employments. That is the mission and purpose of a protective tariff. That is what we mean to maintain, and any measure which will destroy it we shall firmly resist; and if beaten on this floor, we will appeal from your decision to the people, before whom parties and policies must at last be tried. We have free trade among ourselves throughout thirty-eight States and the Territories and among sixty millions of people. Absolute freedom of exchange within our own borders and among our own citizens is the law of the Republic. Reasonable taxation and restraint upon those without is the dictate of enlightened patriotism and the doctrine of the Republican party."— *House of Representatives, May 18, 1888.*

III. The Gorman Tariff.

"*Mr. President and My Fellow Citizens:*— I recall with emotion my last visit to your city.

It was in the political campaign of 1884, when the great leader and statesman of the State of Maine, the beloved by all the country, was the presidential candidate of the Republican party. He was a leader around whom all Ohio Republicans were proud to rally, and to whom they gave a warm, earnest, and cheerful support. He lost the presidency, but could not be deprived of a place in history which that great office, exalted as it is, could not have brightened, and failure to secure which could not blast.

" For, more and better than all else, he has a place in the hearts of the people, as tender and affectionate as that of almost any other American statesman living or dead."

" For eighteen months, my fellow citizens, the Democratic President and Democratic Congress have been running the Government, during which time little else has been running. Industry has been practically stopped. Labor has found little employment, and when employed it has been at greatly reduced wages. Both Government and people have been draining their reserves, and both have been running in debt. The Government has suffered in its revenues and the people in their incomes. The total losses to the country in business, property, and wages are beyond human calculation. There has been no

cessation in the waste of wealth and wages;
no contentment, brightness or hope has anywhere appeared. Discontent and distress have
been universal. The appeals to charity have
never been so numerous and incessant, nor
their necessity everywhere so manifest.

"Congress has disappointed the people,
trifled with the sacred trust confided to it, ex-
cited distrust and disgust among their constit-
uents and impaired their enterprises and invest-
ments. In almost continuous session for thir-
teen months they have done nothing but
aggravate the situation. Pledged, if platforms mean anything, to overthrow our long
continued policy of protection, they have
quarreled and compromised, and, upon their
own testimony, have been compromised.

"The result of their long wrangle is a tariff law with which nobody is satisfied.

"A law which even those who made it apol-
ogize for.

"A law which the chairman of the Committee on Ways and Means and almost the
entire Democratic side of the House condemned by a yea and nay vote only a few
days before its passage, affirming their inten-
tion in the most solemn manner not to permit
it to be enacted.

"A law which was never approved by a
majority of either the House Committee on

Ways and Means or the Senate Committee of Finance, who were charged with the preparation and management of the bill.

" A law which all factions of the Democratic party agree is the work of a monstrous trust, which Chairman Wilson confessed, amid the applause of his confederates, with deep chagrin and humiliation, ' held Congress by the throat.'

" The history of the new tariff legislation is interesting and instructive. The House, which alone has the power to originate revenue bills, passed what is known as the Wilson bill, a measure which has the unenviable distinction of being the only tariff bill in our history that was ever indorsed by a President in his annual message to Congress before it had been reported to the House, and before it had ever been officially adopted by the Ways and Means Committee. It was ostensibly a tariff bill for revenue, and yet on its face it did not raise sufficient revenue to conduct the Government. If that bill had become a law, every estimate I have seen touching its revenue-raising power created an annual deficiency of from $40,000,000 to $60,000,000.

" The bill went to the Senate and took the usual course of reference to the Committee on Finance, which is charged with the revenue legislation of the Senate. After long consideration by the committee, the Wilson bill, with more than four hundred amendments, was reported to the Senate. But after much talking and wrangling it was soon made manifest that neither the Wilson bill, nor the Wilson bill with the Finance Committee's amendments could pass that body.

" And so, taking the matter out of the hands of the Senate and out of the hands of the Finance Committee of the Senate, a self-constituted Adjusting Committee, — a committee unknown to the Constitution, a committee unauthorized by the rules of the Senate or by party caucus or custom, — an Adjusting Committee, consisting of Messrs. Jones of Arkansas, Vest of Missouri, and Harris of Tennessee, undertook to make a bill which would receive the votes of forty-three Senators or a bare majority of all.

" The Democratic party is a most remarkable party. They are for anything to get power, but they are never for anything which got them power.

" They were for free raw materials in the campaign of 1892. But they were opposed to free raw materials after the campaign was successful, and when they possessed the power to make them free.

" They were vociferously opposed to trusts

in their platform and on the stump when they were trying to get back into office. But it is conceded that they became the willing tools and advocates of trusts when opportunity came to strike the blow against them.

"They posed as the true and only friends of labor during the summer and fall of 1892, and even pointed to the Homestead riots as the direct and logical fruits of Republican legislation. But since that time they have inflicted upon American labor the deadliest blow it has received. Their policy had reduced wages and beggared labor beyond description.

"They promised the farmer better prices for his wheat and wool when they were seeking his vote. But when they once obtained his suffrage their economic policy began to force down the prices daily until it has now reached the lowest point known for nearly fifty years.

"They have disappointed every reasonable expectation they raised in the campaign of 1892, but justified every fear or evil prediction urged against them. They have ignored every promise. They have disregarded every obligation. They have broken faith with a trusting people and exposed their insincerity and double dealing. They appear before the American people to-day totally discredited

and in disgrace, upon their own confessions,
before the close of half of the presidential
term. They have utterly failed to redeem any
pledge made to the people, and after more than
a year's continuous session of Congress are
forced to acknowledge their infirmity, imbe-
cility, and the lack of united purpose to carry
out any single one of the great promises of the
campaign. They have exhibited their inherent
weakness and have disclosed irreconcilable
differences with the party.

" The Senate does not agree with the House,
nor the House with the Senate, nor either with
itself or the President, while the great body
of the people is decidedly at variance with all
of them.

" Under such anomalous circumstances, is
it any wonder that President Cleveland, in
his letter to Chairman Wilson, should have
mournfully exclaimed :

"' There is no excuse for mistaking or mis-
apprehending the feeling and the temper of
the rank and file of the Democracy. They
are downcast under the assertion that their
party fails in ability to manage the Government, and they are apprehensive that efforts
to bring about tariff reform may fail : but
they are much more downcast and apprehensive in their fear that Democratic principles
may be surrendered.'

"No party can be safely trusted with the sacred interests of the people or the Government, without it possesses a fixed, honest, and enlightened purpose. Singleness of purpose is necessary to every reform, indispensable to wise administration and legislation. The want of this quality is the infirmity of the present Administration and the present Congress.

"Failure and disappointment were bound to follow an Administration and Congress thus chosen, and the whole country suffers as a result. The Administration and Congress are without compass or rudder. They have at length passed a tariff law, such as it is, but if we credit Democratic testimony alone the people burn with impatience for an opportunity to repudiate both it and them.

"We could bear with resignation their party differences and demoralization if the Democratic party was the sole sufferer. But when we contemplate the widespread ruin to business, and enterprise, and employment, we appreciate the dreadful sacrifice which this Administration has entailed, and the appalling mistake of 1892." *Bangor, Me., Sept. 8, 1894.*

IV.   The Tariff Commission.

"The tariff question has again forced itself into prominence. While it has never ceased

to be a question upon which the political
parties of the country have made some declaration, yet for many years other issues have in
a great measure determined party divisions
and controlled party discipline. The last
presidential campaign brought recognition
and discussion of this issue, and it may be
fairly said that Republican advocacy of the
protective principle contributed in no small
degree to the success of the Republican
national ticket. It can safely be asserted
that the doctrine of a tariff for revenue and
protection as against a tariff for revenue only
is the dominant sentiment in the United
States to-day; and if a vote upon that issue,
with every other question eliminated, could be
had, the majority would not only be large, but
surprisingly large, for the protective principle.

"The Democratic majorities in the Forty-
fourth, Forty-fifth, and Forty-sixth Congresses,
although committed by party utterances and
by platforms as well as the pledges of leaders
to a reduction of duties to a revenue basis,
were unable, with all their party machinery
and the free use of the party lash, to advance
even a step in that direction. Every proposition for a change was met with the almost
solid opposition of this side of the House,
which, with the assistance of a few Representatives on the other side from Pennsyl-

vania and the New England States, was
strong enough to insure, and did insure, the
substantial defeat of every measure looking to
a disturbance of the existing tariff rates.

"Much criticism is indulged in by the
Democratic party upon the enormities of our
tariff, and yet with those years of power, in
absolute control of the House, and a part of
that time controlling the Senate as well, nothing was accomplished by way of removing the
so-called enormities, and at last the party was
compelled to confess that it was unable to
make any progress in that direction.

"This is some evidence at least of the
domination in this country of the protective
idea, or else it demonstrates the infidelity of
the Democratic party to its professed principles; one or the other. I prefer to interpret
the former as its meaning. The sentiment is
surely growing. It has friends to-day that it
never had in the past. Its adherents are no
longer confined to the North and the East,
but are found in the South and in the West.
The idea travels with industry, and is the
associate of enterprise and thrift. It encourages the development of skill, labor, and
inventive genius as part of the great produc-
tive forces. Its advocacy is no longer limited
to the manufacturer, but it has friends the
most devoted among the farmers, the wool

growers, the laborers, and the producers of the land. It is as strong in the country as in the manufacturing towns or the cities; and while it is not taught generally in our colleges, and our young men fresh from universities join with the free-trade thought of the country, practical business and every-day experience later teach them that there are other sources of knowledge besides books, that demonstration is better than theory, and that actual results outweigh an idle philosophy. But, while it is not favored in the colleges, it is taught in the school of experience, in the workshop, where honest men perform an honest day's labor, and where capital seeks the development of national wealth. It is, in my judgment, fixed in our national policy, and no party is strong enough to overthrow it.

" It has become a part of our system, interwoven with our business enterprises everywhere, and is to-day better entitled to be called ' the American system ' than it was in 1824, when Henry Clay christened it with that designation. Fixed as I believe the principle is, the details of an equitable and equal adjustment of the schedule of duties, recognizing fully this idea, fair to all interests, is the work of this House, either through its appropriate committee, or calling to its aid

primarily a commission of experts, as proposed by the bill now under consideration.
My own preference would be that Congress
should do this work, and delegate no part of
it to commissions or committees unknown in
this body. This, however, is a matter of
personal judgment, about which men equally
intelligent and honest, equally devoted to
protection, may differ.

" I can not refrain from saying that we are
taking a new and somewhat hazardous step
in delegating a duty that we ought ourselves to perform — a duty confided to us by
the Constitution, and to no others. It is true
that a commission does not legislate, and,
therefore, its work may or may not be adopted
by Congress. This is the safety of the
proposition. The information it will furnish
will be important, and its statistics of rare
value, but the same sources of information
are open to Congress and to the Committee
on Ways and Means as will be available to
a commission ; and as the former will ulti-
mately have to deal with the question practically in Congress, it has seemed to me, if
that committee were willing to undertake the
task and had the requisite time to perform it,
it would be the wisest and most certain
course to the accomplishment of results de-
sired by all.

"The argument that the proposition for a commission is the suggestion of the protectionists, to secure delay and to postpone present action upon the tariff, comes with bad grace from the party upon the other side of this House. It wasted six years and secured no revision of the tariff. It refused, in the Forty-sixth Congress, to pass the Eaton bill for a tariff commission, which required the report to be made on the first of January last, and which, if they had acted upon it during the closing session of the Forty-sixth Congress, the work of the commission would now have been in the possession of Congress for immediate consideration and practical action. My friend from Kentucky [Mr. Turner], in his speech of March 8, 1882, said :

"'I regard it [a commission] like an affidavit filed in a criminal case, merely for the continuance of a bad cause.'

"If a bad cause, why did not your party abate it when you were in power? If it is an affidavit for a continuance, I beg to remind the gentleman that it was his party which prepared and filed it nearly two years ago, when it had the House and the Senate, and could have disposed of it according to its own liking. Senator Eaton, a distinguished

Democrat, high in the councils of his party, presented the original bill, and for many months it was on the Speaker's desk of a Democratic House, where it was left undisposed of, insuring still further postponement. The Democratic party, and no other, is responsible for the delay, and I charge any injury which delay has produced upon it.

"Mr. Chairman, the wages question as related to the tariff is well illustrated by the following from the Rice Association of Georgia:

"'In the period between 1840 and 1860 the duty on foreign rice was absolutely needless as a protection to the American producer, and valueless as a source of revenue to the Government. The farmer was wholly independent of protection to an industry maintained by labor in cheapness second to that of Asia only, and in effectiveness unsurpassed. By reason of that cheap labor he was in a position to defy competition, and triumphantly met the almost free importation of East India rice, even in the English markets.'

"The *per diem* of slave labor at that time did not much, if at all, exceed twenty cents.

"This fact is the best argument that can be made, and needs no elaboration. It tells the whole story. With slave labor at twenty cents per day, or Asiatic cheap labor, we need no protection, and save for the purposes of revenue our custom-houses might be closed.

When the South depended upon the labor of
its slaves, and employed little or no free labor,
it was as earnest an advocate of free trade as
is England to-day. Now that it must resort
to free labor, it is placed upon the same foot-
ing as Northern producers; it is compelled to
pay a like rate of wages for a day's work, and
therefore demands protection against the
foreign producer, whose product is made or
grown by a cheaper labor. And we find all
through the South a demand for protection to
American industry against a foreign competition, bent upon their destruction and determined to possess the American market.

" But our laboring men are not content with
the hedger's and ditcher's rate of pay. No
worthy American wants to reduce the price
of labor in the United States. It ought not
to be reduced; for the sake of the laborer and
his family and the good of society it ought to
be maintained. To increase it would be
in better harmony with the public sense.
Our labor must not be debased, nor our laborers degraded to the level of slaves, nor any
pauper or servile system in any form, nor
under any guise whatsoever, at home or
abroad. Our civilization will not permit it.
Our humanity forbids it. Our traditions are
opposed to it. The stability of our institutions rests upon the contentment and intelli-

gence of all our people, and these can only
be possessed by maintaining the dignity of
labor and securing to it its just rewards.
That protection opens new avenues for employment, broadens and diversifies the field
of labor, and presents variety of vocation, is
manifest from our own experience.

" Free trade may be suitable to Great Brit-
tain and its peculiar social and political structure, but it has no place in this Republic,
where classes are unknown and where caste
has long since been banished ; where equality
is the rule ; where labor is dignified and honorable ; where education and improvement
are the individual striving of every citizen,
no matter what may be the accident of his
birth or the poverty of his early surroundings.
Here the mechanic of to-day is the manufacturer of a few years hence. Under such conditions, free trade can have no abiding-place
here. We are doing very well; no other
nation has done better, or makes a better
showing in the world's balance-sheet. We
ought to be satisfied with the progress thus
far made, and contented with our outlook for
the future. We know what we have done and
what we can do under the policy of protection. We have had some experience with a
revenue tariff, which neither inspires hope,
nor courage, nor confidence. Our own his-

tory condemns the policy we oppose, and is
the best vindication of the policy which we
advocate. It needs no other. It furnished
us in part the money to prosecute the war for
the Union to a successful termination ; it has
assisted largely in furnishing the revenue to
meet our great public expenditures and dimin
ish with unparalleled rapidity our great national debt ; it has contributed in securing
to us an unexampled credit ; it has developed
the resources of the country and quickened
the energies of our people ; it has made us
what the nation should be, independent and
self - reliant; it has made us industrious in
peace, and secured us independence in war ;
and we find ourselves in the beginning of the
second century of the Republic without a
superior in industrial arts, without an equal in
commercial prosperity, with a sound financial
system, with an overflowing treasury, blessed
at home and at peace with all mankind. Shall
we reverse the policy which has rewarded us
with such magnificent results? Shall we aban-
don the policy which, pursued for twenty
years, has produced such unparalleled growth
and prosperity ?

"No, no. Let us, Mr. Chairman, pass this
bill. The creation of a commission will give
no alarm to business, will menace no industry
in the United States. Whatever of good it

brings to us on the first Monday in December
next we can accept ; all else we can and will
reject." *House of Representatives, April 6,
1882.*

V   What Protection Means to Virginia.

" *My Fellow Citizens :*—I come to your State
upon the invitation of the Chairman of the
Republican State Committee, to talk to you
about the country and its condition, and the
relation of the two political parties to our
present and future.   I do not come to tell you
the splendid story of the Republican party in
the past, for with that you are all familiar.   I
come rather to talk to you of the future, of
that which concerns your labor, your material
interests, and your individual as well as the
general prosperity.   I come to say in Virginia
precisely what I have said in Ohio, for there
is one thing that can always be said about the
Republican party — it is a national party.   It
advocates the same principles in Ohio and
Massachusetts, in New York and New Jersey,
that it advocates in Virginia, Mississippi, and
North and South Carolina ; for wherever you
find Republicans, whether it is in one of the
States of the North, or in one of the States
of the South, you find them always standing
upon the same platform, always carrying the

same flag, always in favor of national unity and national prosperity.

"A great question, my fellow citizens, before this country — a question of the now and a question of the hereafter — is whether we shall have maintained in the United States a system of protection to American labor and American development, or whether we shall have practical free trade with all the countries of the world, and impose no duties except for revenue upon articles of merchandise, and products that may be brought into the United States. No, we want no free trade. First of all, we want to know which party, if any, is in favor of free trade? And which party is in favor of a protective tariff? You say that the Democratic party is in favor of free trade, and the Republican party in favor of protection. But there are a good many Democrats who say they are in favor of protection. There are two ways of determining the position of a political party: one is by its platforms, the other is by its record and its votes in the Congress of the United States.

" Let us try the Democratic and Republican parties by this test for a moment, because I would not do the Democratic party any injustice upon this subject if I could ; and I assert here to-night, and I challenge contradiction by any gentleman in this audience, or elsewhere,

that since 1840, and before, with just two
exceptions, the Democratic party of the
United States in national conventions and in
national platforms, from 1840 to 1884, has
declared in favor of a revenue tariff closely
approximating free trade.   They did it in
1840, they did it in 1844, they did it in 1848,
they did it in 1852, they did it in 1856, they did it
in 1860, and again in 1868, with a suggestion of
'incidental protection,' and they omitted it in
1864 and 1872.   And why did they omit it?
They omitted it in 1872, because in that year the
Democratic party nominated for its presidential candidate the old Republican leader,
Horace Greeley, who had taught the younger
men of this country the great doctrine of
American protection, and they did not, therefore, that year dare to declare in favor of free
trade with a protectionist standing on their
platform.

   " Now, my fellow citizens, what is this tariff?   It is very largely misunderstood, or,
rather, it is very little understood, and, if I
can to-night make this audience, the humblest
and the youngest in it, understand what the
tariff means, I will feel that I have been well
paid for my trip to Virginia.   What then is
the tariff?   The tariff, my fellow citizens, is a
tax put upon goods made outside of the
United States, and brought into the United

States for sale and consumption. That is, we say to England, we say to Germany, we say to France, 'If you want to sell your goods to the people of the United States, you must pay so much for the privilege of doing it; you must pay so much per ton, so much per yard, so much per foot, as the case may be, for the privilege of selling to the American people, and what you pay in that form, goes into the public treasury to help discharge the public burdens.' It is just like the little city of Petersburg, for example. I do not know what your customs may be, but in many cities of the North, if a man comes to our cities and wants to sell goods to our people on the street, not to occupy any of our business houses, not being a permanent resident or trader, not living there, but travelling and selling from town to town, if he comes to one of our little cities in Ohio, we say to him: 'Sir, you must pay so much into the city treasury for the privilege of selling goods to our people here.' Now, why do we do that? We do it to protect our own merchants.

"Just so our Government says to the countries of the Old World; it says to England and the rest: 'If you want to come in and sell to our people, you must pay something for the privilege of doing it, and pay it at the Treasury and at the custom-houses,' and that goes into the Treasury of the United States to help discharge the public debt and pay the current expenses of the Government. Now, that is the tariff, and if any man at this point wants to ask me any questions about it, I want him to do it now, for I don't want, when I am gone, to have some Democrat say, ' If I could only have had an opportunity to ask him a question, I would like to have done it, because I could have exposed the fallacy of his argument.'   So I want him to do it now.

" I said to the people of Ohio, when we were making our canvass this year, ' Elect a Republican Legislature, so that we may send John Sherman back to the Senate of the United States, and thereby preserve a Republican majority in that great parliamentary body.'   And I say to the citizens of Virginia, I do not care what your politics are, I do not care where you stood during the great Civil War, if you are interested in the development of a new and progressive order of things in Virginia,—I say to you, as I said to the people of Ohio, ' Elect a Legislature that will send to the Senate of the United States a man who will vote for a protective tariff,' and who has done it over and over again, and if you do that, the Republican party will preserve its majority in that great body, which is the only Republican citadel we have left.

The House is Democratic; the President is
Democratic, or they think he is. They
thought he was, but I do not know how he
is going to turn out. They have the House
and the President, and if General Mahone is
defeated in Virginia, I do not know that it is
possible for the Republicans to preserve the
Senate during the entire administration of
Grover Cleveland.

"Now, my fellow citizens, a little more
about the tariff. It is a very dry subject,
but it is a subject which affects your purse,
your dress, your living, and your homes; it
affects your every-day interests, and your
ability to live in comfort, and to keep your
family from want.

"Why, they call me a high protectionist;
I am a high protectionist; I do not deny
it, and I would not be seriously disturbed
in mind if the tariff were a little higher.
Do you know of any reason in the world
why Americans should not make everything that Americans need? There is, indeed, no reason. We have the capital; we
have the skill; we have all the elements of
Nature; we have everything we need, and I
would make the duty so high that there would
be fewer English goods coming into the
United States and more American goods consumed at home. Do you think there would

be an idle man in America if we manufactured everything that Americans used? Do you think if we did n't buy anything from abroad at all, but made everything we needed, that every man would not be employed in the United States, and employed at a profitable remuneration? Why, everybody is benefited by protection, even the people who do not believe in it — for they get great benefit out of it, but will not confess it; and that is what is the matter with Virginia. Heretofore, she has not believed in it. You have not had a public man that I know of in Washington for twenty-five years, save one, except the Republicans, who did not vote against the great doctrine of American protection, American industries, and American labor; and do you imagine that anybody is coming to Virginia with his money to build a mill, or a factory, or a furnace, and develop your coal and your ore, bring his money down here, when you vote every time against his interests — and don't let those who favor them vote at all? No. If you think so, you might just as well be undeceived now, for they will not come.

"Why, old John Randolph, I don't know how many years ago, said on the floor of the American Congress, in opposing a protective tariff, 'he did not believe in manufactories.' Why,' said he, 'if you have manufactories in

Philadelphia, you will have cholera six months in the year.' That was what the 'Sage of Roanoke' said, and Virginia seems to be still following the sentiments he uttered years and years ago.

"I tell you, manufactories do not bring cholera — they bring coin, coin; coin for the poor man, coin for the rich, coin for everybody who will work, comfort and contentment for all deserving people. And, if you vote for increasing manufactories, my fellow citizens, you will vote for the best interests of your own State, and you will be making iron, and steel, and pottery, and all the great leading products, just as Ohio and Pennsylvania are making them to-day.

"Tell me why your land in Virginia, in 1880, was worth an average price of but $10.92 all over the State, while over in Pennsylvania the average price per acre was $49. Virginia has just as good soil as Pennsylvania. Virginia has just as rich minerals as Pennsylvania, and what makes the difference between the $11 and $49 is, that you have little development in Virginia — and your old policy will never bring more.

"Stand by your interests — stand by the party that stands by the people. Because in the Republican party there is no such thing as class or caste. The humble, poor colored man in the Republican party, the humble, poor white man in the Republican party, has an equal chance with the opulent white or colored Republican in the race of life. And so with every race, and every nationality, the Republican party says, ' Come up higher!' We do not appeal to passions; we do not appeal to baser instincts; we do not appeal to race or war prejudices. We do appeal to your consciences; we do appeal to your own best interests, to stand by a party that stands by the people. Vote the Republican ticket, stand by the protective policy, stand by American industries, stand by that policy which believes in American work for American workmen, that believes in American wages for American laborers, that believes in American homes for American citizens. Vote to maintain that system by which you can earn enough not only to give you the comforts of life, but the refinements of life; enough to educate and equip your children, who may not have been fortunate by birth, who may not have been born with a silver spoon in their mouths; enough to enable them in turn to educate and prepare their children for the great possibilities of American life. I am for America, because America is for the common people. We have no kings, we have no dukes, we have no lords.

Every man in this country represents the sovereign power of this great Government, and every man has equal power with every other man to clothe that sovereign with his will. I believe in America, because we have no laws in this country like the old laws of primogeniture, where everything goes to the first-born; and I like this country for another thing: When the rich man dies he cannot entail his property. Often the boy he leaves behind him, reared in luxury and wealth, if raised to do nothing, can not take care of the property left him. I will tell you how it is up in our country, and I want it so down here in Virginia. In less than twenty-five years the son of a poor man has a part of the wealth which the opulent ancestor left that will not stay with his unworthy descendant. And so everybody gets a chance after a while. The wealthy men of our country to-day were poor men forty years ago, and the future manufacturers are the mechanics of the present. Make that possible in Virginia, and you will win. Make it possible to break down the prejudices of the past. Get out from under your ancestral tree. Recognize and give force to the Constitution, permit every man to vote for the party of his choice, and have his ballot honestly counted. Push to the front where you belong as a State and a people.

" Be assured that the Republicans of the North harbor no resentments — only ask for the results of the war. They wish you the highest prosperity and greatest development. They bid you, in the language of Whittier:

" ' A schoolhouse plant on every hill
Stretching in radiate nerve-lines thence,
The quick wires of intelligence ;
Till North and South together brought
Shall own the same electric thought ;
In peace a common flag salute,
And, side by side in labor's free
And unresentful rivalry,
Harvest the fields wherein they fought.' "

— *Petersburg, Va., Oct. 29, 1885.*

VI. The McKinley Tariff of 1890.

" I do not intend to enter upon any extended discussion of the two economic systems which divide parties in this House and the people throughout the country. For two years we have been occupied in both branches of Congress and in our discussions before the people with these contending theories of taxation.

" At the first session of the Fiftieth Congress the House spent several weeks in an elaborate and exhaustive discussion of these systems. The Senate was for as many weeks engaged in their investigation and in debate

upon them, while in the political contest of
1888 the tariff in all its phases was the absorbing question, made so by the political
platforms of the respective parties, to the
exclusion, practically, of every other subject
of party division. It may be said that, from
the December session of 1887–'88 to March
4, 1889, no public question ever received, in
Congress and out, such scrutinizing investigation as that of the tariff. It has, therefore,
seemed to me that any lengthy general discussion of these principles at this time, so
soon after their thorough consideration and
determination by the people, is neither
expected, required, nor necessary.

"If any one thing was settled by the election of 1888, it was that the protective policy,
as promulgated in the Republican platform
and heretofore inaugurated and maintained
by the Republican party, should be secured
in any fiscal legislation to be had by the Congress chosen in that great contest and upon
that mastering issue. I have interpreted that
victory to mean, and the majority in this
House and in the Senate to mean, that a
revision of the tariff is not only demanded
by the votes of the people, but that such revision should be on the line and in full
recognition of the principle and purpose of
protection. The people have spoken ; they

want their will registered and their decree
embodied in public legislation. The bill
which the Committee on Ways and Means
has presented is their answer and interpreta-
tion of that victory and in accordance with
its spirit and letter and purpose. We have
not been compelled to abolish the internal
revenue system that we might preserve the
protective system, which we were pledged to
do in the event that the abolition of the one
was essential to the preservation of the other.
That was unnecessary.

" It is asserted in the views of the minority,
submitted with the report accompanying this
bill, that the operation of the bill will not
diminish the revenues of the Government; that
with the increased duties we have imposed
upon foreign articles which may be sent to
market here we have increased taxation, and
that, therefore, instead of being a diminution of
the revenues of the Government, there will be
an increase in the sum of $50,000,000 or $60,-
000,000. Now, that statement is entirely mis-
leading. It can only be accepted upon the
assumption that the importation of the present
year under this bill, if it becomes a law, will
be equal to the importations of like articles
under the existing law; and there is not a
member of the Committee on Ways and
Means, there is not a member of the minority

of that Committee, there is not a member of
the House on either side, who does not know
that the very instant that you have increased
the duties to a fair protective point, putting
them above the highest revenue point, that
very instant you diminish importations and to
that extent diminish the revenue. Nobody
can well dispute this proposition. Why, when
the Senate bill was under consideration by the
Committee on Ways and Means, over which
my friend from Texas presided in the last
Congress, the distinguished chairman of that
committee [Mr. Mills] wrote a letter to Secretary Fairchild inquiring what would be the
effect of increased duties proposed under the
Senate bill, and this is Mr. Fairchild's reply:

"'Where the rates upon articles successfully produced
here are materially increased, it is fair to assume that
the imports of such articles would decrease and the
revenue therefrom diminish.'

" He further states that where the rate upon an article is so increased as to deprive the
foreign producer of the power to compete with
the domestic producer, the revenue from that
source will cease altogether. Secretary Fairchild only states what has been the universal
experience in the United States wherever increase of duties above the revenue point has
been made upon articles which we can pro-

duce in the United States. Therefore, it is
safe to assume that no increase of the revenues, taking the bill through, will arise from
the articles upon which duties have been advanced. Now as to the schedules:

"The bill recommends the retention of the
present rates of duty on earthen and china-
ware. No other industry in the United States
either deserves or requires the fostering care
of Government more than this one. It is a
business requiring technical and artistic
knowledge, and the most careful attention to
the many and delicate processes through
which the raw material must pass to the completed product. For many years, down to
1863, the pottery industry of the United
States had very little or no success, and made
but slight progress in a practical and commercial way. At the close of the low-tariff
period of 1860, there was but one pottery in
the United States, with two small kilns.
There were no decorating kilns at the time.
In 1873, encouraged by the tariff and the
gold premium, which was an added protection,
we had increased to 20 potteries, with 68
kilns, but still no decorating kilns. The capital invested was $1,020,000, and the value of
the product was $1,180,000. In 1882, there
were 55 potteries, 244 kilns, 26 decorating
kilns, with a capital invested of $5,076,000,

and an annual product of $5,299,140. The wages paid in the potteries in 1882 were $2,387,000, and the number of employés engaged therein 7,000; the ratio of wages to sales, in 1882, was 45 per cent. In 1889, there were 80 potteries, 401 kilns, and decorating kilns had increased from 26 in 1822, to 188 in 1889. The capital invested in the latter year was $10,957,357, the value of the product was $10,389,910, amount paid in wages, $6,265,224, and the number of employés engaged, 16,900. The ratio of wages to sales was 60 per cent. of decorated ware and 50 per cent. of white ware. The per cent. of wages to value of product, it will be observed, has advanced from 45 per cent. in 1882, to 60 per cent. in 1889. This increase is not due, as might be supposed, to an advance in wages, but results in a reduction in the selling price of the product and the immense increase in sales of decorated ware in which labor enters in greater proportion to materials. The total importation for 1874 and 1875 of earthenware was to the value of $4,441,216, and in 1888 and 1889 it ran up to $6,476,190. The American ware produced in 1889 was valued at $10,389,910. The difference between the wages of labor in this country and competing countries in the manufacture of earthenware is fully 100 per cent.

"The agricultural condition of the country has received the careful attention of the committee, and every remedy which was believed to be within the power of tariff legislation to give has been granted by this bill. The depression in agriculture is not confined to the United States. The reports of the Agricultural Department indicate that this distress is general; that Great Britain, France, and Germany are suffering in a larger degree than the farmers of the United States. Mr. Dodge, statistician of the department, says, in his report of March, 1890, that the depression in agriculture in Great Britain has probably been more severe than that of any other nation; which would indicate that it is greater even in a country whose economic system differs from ours, and that this condition is inseparable from any fiscal system, and less under the protective than the revenue tariff system.

"It has been asserted in the views of the minority that the duty put upon wheat and other agricultural products would be of no value to the agriculturists of the United States. The committee, believing differently, has advanced the duty upon these products. As we are the greatest wheat-producing country of the world, it is habitually asserted and believed by many that this product is safe from foreign competition. We do not appreciate that while the United States last year raised 490,000,000 bushels of wheat, France raised 316,000,000 bushels, Italy raised 103,000,000 bushels, Russia 189,000,000 bushels, and India 243,000,000 bushels, and that the total production of Asia, including Asia Minor, Persia, and Syria, amounted to over 315,000,000 bushels. Our sharpest competition comes from Russia and India, and the increased product of other nations only serves to increase the world's supply, and diminish proportionately the demand for ours; and if we will only reflect on the difference between the cost of labor in producing wheat in the United States and in competing countries, we will readily perceive how near we are to the danger line, if indeed we have not quite reached it, so far even as our own markets are concerned.

" Prof. Goldwin Smith, a Canadian and political economist, speaking of the Canadian farmers and the effect of this bill upon their interests, says:

" 'They will be very much injured if the McKinley bill shall be adopted. The agricultural schedule will bear very hardly on the Canadian farmers who particularly desire to find a market in the United States for their eggs, their barley, and their horses. The European market is of little value to them for their horses. If there shall be a slow market in England all the

profits will be consumed on a cargo of horses and
great loss will entail. I do not see how the Canadian
farmers can export their produce to the United States
if the McKinley bill shall become a law.'

"If that be true, Mr. Chairman, then the
annual exports of about $25,000,000 in agri-
cultural products will be supplied to the
people of the United States by the American
farmer rather than by the Canadian farmer;
and who will say that $25,000,000 of addi-
tional demand for American agricultural
products will not inure to the benefit of the
American farmer; and that $25,000,000 dis-
tributed among our own farmers will not
relieve some of the depression now prevailing,
and give to the farmer confidence and increased ability to lift the mortgages from his
lands?

"The duty recommended in the bill is not
alone to correct this inequality, but to make
the duty on foreign tin plate high enough to
insure its manufacture in this country to the
extent of our home consumption. The only
reason we are not doing it now and have not
been able to do it in the past is because of
inadequate duties. We have demonstrated
our ability to make it here as successfully as
they do in Wales. We have already made it
here. Two factories were engaged in producing tin plate in the years 1873, 1874, and

1875, but no sooner had they got fairly under
way than the foreign manufacturer reduced
his price to a point which made it impossible
for our manufacturers to continue. When
our people embarked in the business foreign
tin plate was selling for $12 per box, and to
crush them out, before they were firmly
established, the price was brought down to
$4.50 per box; but it did not remain there.
When the fires were put out in the American
mills, and its manufacture thought by the
foreigners to be abandoned, the price of tin
plate advanced, until in 1879 it was selling
for $9 and $10 a box. Our people again tried
it, and again the prices were depressed, and
again our people abandoned temporarily the
enterprise, and, as a gentleman stated before
the committee, twice they have lost their
whole investment through the combination of
the foreign manufacturers in striking down
the prices, not for the benefit of the consumer, but to drive our manufacturers from
the business; and this would be followed by
an advance within six months after our mills
were shut down.

"We propose this advanced duty to protect
our manufacturers and consumers against the
British monopoly, in the belief that it will
defend our capital and labor in the production
of tin plate until they shall establish an indus-

try which the English will recognize has come to stay, and then competition will insure regular and reasonable prices to consumers. It may add a little temporarily to the cost of tin plate to the consumer, but will eventuate in steadier and more satisfactory prices. At the present prices for foreign tin plate, the proposed duty would not add anything to the cost of the heavier grades of tin to the consumer. If the entire duty was added to the cost of the can it would not advance it more than one-third or one-half of one cent, for on a dozen fruit-cans the addition would properly only be about three cents.

" Mr. Chairman, gentlemen on the other side take great comfort in a quotation which they make from Daniel Webster. They have thought it so valuable that they have put it in their minority report. It is from a speech made by Mr. Webster in Faneuil Hall in 1820 when he condemned the protective policy. I want to put Daniel Webster in 1846 against Daniel Webster in 1820. Listen to an extract from his speech of July 25, 1846 — the last tariff speech and probably the most elaborate tariff speech that he ever made in his long public career. He then said :

" 'But, sir, before I proceed further, I will take notice of what appears to be some attempt, latterly, by the republication of opinions and expressions, arguments and speeches of mine, at an earlier and a later period of my life, to place me in a position of inconsistency on this subject of the protective policy of the country. Mr. President, if it be an inconsistency to hold an opinion upon a subject of public policy to-day in one state of circumstances, and to hold a different opinion upon the same subject of public policy to-morrow in a different state of circumstances, if that be an inconsistency, I admit its applicability to myself.'

" And then, after discussing the great benefits of the protective tariff, he added :

"' The interest of every laboring community requires diversity of occupations, pursuits, and objects of industry. The more that diversity is multiplied or extended the better. To diversify employment is to increase employment and to enhance wages. And, sir, take this great truth ; place it on the title-page of every book of political economy intended for the use of the Government ; put it in every farmer's almanac ; let it be the heading of the column in every mechanic's magazine ; proclaim it everywhere, and make it a proverb, that where there is work for the hands of men there will be work for their teeth. Where there is employment there will be bread. It is a great blessing to the poor to have cheap food, but greater than that, prior to that, and of still higher value, is the blessing of being able to buy food by honest and respectable employment. Employment feeds, and clothes, and instructs. Employment gives health, sobriety, and morals. Constant employment and well-paid labor produce in a country like ours general prosperity, contentment, and cheerfulness. Thus happy have we seen the country. Thus happy may we long continue to see it.'

" In this happy condition we have seen the country under a protective policy. It is hoped we may long continue to see it, and if he had lived long enough he would have seen the best vindication of his later views. Then he continued, and I commend this especially, in all kindness and with great respect, to the gentlemen of the minority of the committee :

"' I hope I know more of the Constitution of my country than I did when I was twenty years old.

"' I hope I have contemplated its great objects more broadly. I hope I have read with deeper interest the sentiments of the great men who framed it. I hope I have studied with more care the condition of the country when the Convension assembled to form it. . . . And now, sir, allow me to say that I am quite indifferent, or rather thankful, to those conductors of the public press who think they cannot do better than now and then to spread my poor opinions before the public.'

" What is the nature of the complaint against this bill — that it shuts us out of the foreign market ? No, for whatever that is worth to our citizens will be just as accessible under this bill as under the present law. We place no tax or burden or restraint upon American products going out of the country. They are as free to seek the best markets as the products of any commercial power, and as free to go out as though we had absolute free trade.

Statistics show that protective tariffs have not interrupted our export trade, but that it has always steadily and largely increased under them.

" In the year 1843, being the first year after the protective tariff of 1842 went into operation, our exports exceeded our imports $40,-392,229, and in the following year they exceeded our imports $3,141,226. In the two years following the excess of exports over imports was $15,475,000. The last year under that tariff the excess of exports over imports was $34,317,249. So during the five years of the tariff of 1842 the excess of exports over imports was $62,175,000. Under the low tariff of 1846, this was reversed, and, with the single exception of the year 1858, the imports exceeded the exports (covering a period of fourteen years) $465,553,625.

" We have now enjoyed twenty-nine years continuously of protective tariff laws — the longest uninterrupted period in which that policy has prevailed since the formation of the Federal Government — and we find ourselves at the end of that period in a condition of independence and prosperity the like of which has never been witnessed at any other period in the history of our country, and the like of which has no parallel in the recorded history of the world. In all that goes to make a nation great and strong and independent we have made extraordinary strides. In arts, in science, in literature, in manufactures, in invention, in scientific principles applied to manufacture and agriculture, in wealth and credit and national honor we are at the very front, abreast with the best, and behind none.

"In 1860, after fourteen years of a revenue tariff, just the kind of a tariff that our political adversaries are advocating to-day, the business of the country was prostrated, agriculture was deplorably depressed, manufacturing was on the decline, and the poverty of the Government itself made this nation a byword in the financial centres of the world. We neither had money nor credit. Both are essential; a nation can get on if it has abundant revenues, but if it has none it must have credit. We had neither, as the legacy of the Democratic revenue tariff. We have both now. We have a surplus revenue and a spotless credit. I need not state what is so fresh in our minds, so recent in our history as to be known to every gentleman who hears me, that from the inauguration of the protective tariff laws of 1861, the old Morrill tariff — which has brought to that veteran statesman the highest honor, and will give to him his proudest monument — this condition changed. Confidence was restored, courage was inspired, the Government started upon a progressive era under a system thoroughly American.

"With a great war on our hands, with an army to enlist and prepare for service, with untold millions of money to supply, the pro tective tariff never failed us in a single emergency, and while money was flowing into our treasury to save the Government, industries were springing up all over the land — the foundation and corner-stone of our prosperity and glory. With a debt of over $2,750,000,000 when the war terminated, holding on to our protective laws, against Democratic opposition, we have reduced that debt at an average rate of more than $62,000,000 each year, $174,000 every twenty-four hours for the last twenty-five years, and what looked to be a burden almost impossible to bear has been removed, under the Republican fiscal system, until now it is less than $1,000,000,000, and with the payment of this vast sum of money the nation has not been impoverished. The individual citizen has not been burdened or bankrupted. National and individual prosperity have gone steadily on, until our wealth is so great as to be almost incomprehensible when put into figures.

" First, then, to retain our own market, under the Democratic system of raising revenue by removing all protection, would require our producers to sell at as low a price and upon as favorable terms as our foreign competitors. How could that be done? In one way only — by producing as cheaply as those who would seek our markets. What would that entail? An entire revolution in the methods and condition and conduct of business here, a leveling down through every channel, to the lowest line of our competitors; our habits of living would have to be changed, our wages cut down fifty per cent. more, our comfortable homes exchanged for hovels, our independence yielded up, our citizenship demoralized. These are conditions inseparable to free trade; these would be necessary if we would command our own market among our own people; and if we would invade the world's markets, harsher conditions and greater sacrifices would be demanded of the masses. Talk about depression — we would then have it in its fulness. We would revel in unrestrained trade. Everything would, indeed, be cheap, but how costly when measured by the degradation which would ensue! When merchandise is the cheapest, men are the poorest, and the most distressing experiences in the history of our country — aye, in all human history — have been when everything was the lowest and cheapest, measured by gold, for everything was the highest and the dearest, measured by labor. We want no return of cheap times in our own country. We have no wish to adopt the conditions of other nations. Experience has demonstrated that for us and ours, and for the present and the future, the protective system meets our wants, our conditions, promotes the national design, and will work out our destiny better than any other.

"With me, this position is a deep conviction, not a theory. I believe in it and thus warmly advocate it because enveloped in it are my country's highest development and greatest prosperity ; out of it come the greatest gains to the people, the greatest comforts to the masses, the widest encouragement for manly aspirations, with the largest rewards, dignifying and elevating our citizenship, upon which the safety, and purity, and permanency of our political system depend."— *House of Representatives, May 7, 1890.*

CHAPTER III.

THE PURITY OF THE BALLOT.

AT the foundation of a republican government rests a pure, intelligent, and untramelled ballot. This has always been McKinley's idea, and while deprecating any survival of sectional animosities, he rigidly insists that the free ballot of the Constitution shall be guaranteed to the nation's humblest citizens.

I. The War Is Over.

' THE war is over, the flag of the lost and wicked cause went down at Appomattox more than twenty years ago; but that does not prevent us from insisting that all that was gained in war shall not be lost in peace. The contest is over — we pray never to be resumed; but that which was secured by so much blood, suffering, and sacrifice must be cheerfully accorded by every patriotic citizen. The struggle cost too much human life and public treasure to be apologized for, or frittered away, under any pretext. The results admit of no compromise. The standard of patriotism and the respect for law must not be lowered; the hideous spectre of a wicked conspiracy need not be veiled. Patriotism and obedience to the Constitution, the old as well as the new, must be kept to the forefront. Weak and sentimental gush must not be permitted to conceal disobedience of the law, or protect the flagrant violators of the rights of citizenship. The country's enemies were forgiven long ago, liberal and magnanimous pardon was extended to them. Mutual forbearance should be cultivated, honorable concessions were made upon both sides, but the freedom and political equality of all men must be fully and honorably recognized wherever our flag floats." — *Campaign speech at Ironton, O., Oct. 1, 1885.*

II. The Black Color-bearer.

"Our black allies must neither be deserted nor forsaken. Every right secured them by the Constitution must be as surely given to them as though God had put upon their faces the color of the Anglo-Saxon race. They fought for the flag in the war, and that flag, with all it represents and stands for, must secure them every constitutional right in peace. At Baton Rouge, the first regiment of the Black Brigade, before starting for Port Hudson, received at the hands of its white colonel — Colonel Stafford — its regimental colors in a speech from the colonel, which ended with this injunction:

"'Color-bearer, guard, defend, protect, die for, but do not surrender, these colors.'

"To which the sergeant replied — and he was as black as my coat:

"'Colonel, I'll return those flags to you in honor, or I'll report to God the reason why.'

"He fell mortally wounded, in one of the desperate charges in front of Port Hudson, with his face to the enemy, with those colors in his clenched fist pressed upon his breast. He did not return the colors, but the God above him knew the reason why.

"Against those who fought on the other side in that great conflict we have no resentment; for them we have no bitterness. We would impose upon them no punishment; we would inflict upon them no indignity. They are our brothers. We would save them even from humiliation. But I will tell you what we insist upon, and we will insist upon it until it is secured — that the settlement made between Grant and Lee at Appomattox, which was afterward embodied in the Constitution of the United States, shall be obeyed and respected in every part of this Union. More we have never asked, less we will not have." — *New York, "The American Volunteer Soldier," May 30, 1889.*

III.   Fair Elections.

"*Mr. Chairman:* — The first movement in the programme of a restored Democracy has already been accomplished, so far as this House is concerned, in the paralyzation of the executive force to preserve peace at the polls. The second step in the same programme is only checked by a few intervening days, when the purity of the ballot-box is to be submitted to the same lawlessness, with no power in the Federal head to insure or preserve it.

"The proposition offered by Mr. Southard in the closing hours of the Forty-fifth Congress, and for the most part now renewed in the extraordinary session of the present Congress, to repeal certain sections of the statutes of the United States known as the Federal election laws, is a bold and wanton attempt to wipe from the law all protection of the ballot-box, and surrender its purity to the unholy hand of the hired repeater, and its control to the ballot-box stuffers of the great cities of the North and the tissue-ballot party of the South.

"So determined is the Democratic party in the House to break down these wise and just measures, intended to secure an honest ballot to the legal voter, that they make them a rider to an important appropriation bill, making them, in the language of my colleague [Mr. McMahon], 'a necessary companion to the money voted in the bill.'

"The repeal of these laws will remove every safeguard against fraud in the exercise of the elective franchise, and will again make possible the enormous outrages upon a pure ballot and free government which marked the elections in the city of New York and elsewhere in 1868, the wickedness and extent of which made existing laws necessary and imperative. The proposition we are now considering is an open assault upon the freedom and purity of elections.

"Article I. of the Constitution declares:

"'The times, places, and manner of holding elections for Senators and Representatives shall be prescribed in each State by the Legislature thereof; but the Congress may at any time by law make or alter such regulations, except as to the places of choosing Senators.'

"This constitutional provision confers upon Congress full and adequate power at any time to make or alter times, places, and manner of holding elections for Representatives, and to make or alter such regulations.

"The Democratic party has thus abandoned the constitutional objection by allowing the sections in relation to supervisors of elections,

with some limitations, to remain. They surrender the constitutional doctrine so strenuously urged against existing law. My
distinguished friend from Ohio [Mr. Hurd],
and the gentleman from Kentucky [Mr.
Carlisle], who addressed the Committee
yesterday, seem not to have been present at
the last caucus of their party, for their arguments are wholly based upon the constitutional
question. Let me suggest to my friends that
if the law is unconstitutional the courts are
open to them, where that question can be
judicially determined for all time ; and let me
remind them that this law has been on the
statute-book for now seven years, and the
question they make, although decided ad-
versely to their theory by an inferior court,
has never found its way to the final tribunal
in such cases — the Supreme Court of the
United States. To that tribunal we invite
them to go. I repeat, that permitting the
supervisors' law to stand is a giving away of
all constitutional objection to the entire body
of the law. It explodes the old dogma of
State rights, and removes all necessity for any
discussion upon that point.

" Enough of the law is left to recognize the
principle always contended for by the Republican party, that Congress had the power and
that it was its plain duty to guard and protect

elections where its own members were to be chosen to seats in this body ; but while admitting the constitutional right, they are careful to wipe out all the provisions which give such a law practical effect in securing an honest election and preventing force and fraud at the polls. They are in favor of the law, but opposed to its execution.

*   *   *   *   *

" I have tried fairly to meet and answer the principal objections urged to this law. Are there any others? In the discussion had in the Forty-fifth Congress much stress was placed upon the great expense attending the execution of the law. I learn that at Cincinnati. in my own State, the expense of deputy marshals. in 1878. was less than $400, and they never had a fairer, purer election than at that time. But to this, in general terms, I answer, What signifies the cost, if thereby we can secure a free and fair ballot in this country? Who will count the cost. if the enforcement of this law will prevent the repeaters and moonshiners from controlling the elections and subverting the popular will? For involved in this proposition is the existence of the Republic and the perpetuation of republican institutions. If honest, fair elections can not be had, free government is a farce; it is no longer the popular will which is supreme.

Free government can not be estimated by dollars nor measured by cost. We have long ago discarded that consideration. This objection has been urged many times before to the enforcement of great fundamental doctrines and principles. The same objection was urged to the prosecution of the war for the preservation of the Union and free government. Public sentiment did not listen then to the cry of cost; it hesitated not, it faltered not then; it ignored the cost; it fought and successfully fought the great battle of freedom; and public sentiment will not now pause to count the paltry cost, when free and fair elections, the foundation-stone of free government, are involved in the threatened danger. If I do not misjudge, the people who fought for free government and maintained it at so great a cost will now be found firm and invincible for a free ballot and fair elections. Let me remind the other side of this Chamber that supervisors and marshals will not be needed, and therefore no cost will be incurred, whenever the party which employs tissue ballots and drives colored citizens from the polls shall do so no more forever, and whenever Democratic repeaters shall cease to corrupt the ballot — the great fountain of power in this country; in a single sentence, whenever, throughout this whole country, in every State thereof, citizenship is respected and the rights under it are fully and amply secured; when every citizen who is entitled to vote shall be secure in the free exercise of that right, and the ballot-box shall be protected from illegal voters, from fraud and violence, Federal supervisors of Federal elections will be neither expensive nor oppressive.

" Has any legal voter in the United States been prevented from exercising his right of suffrage by this law, or by the officers acting under it? This is the practical question. None that I have ever heard of ; while thousands, yes, tens of thousands of illegal voters have been deterred from voting by virtue of it. The honest voter has no fear of this law; it touches him as lightly as the law of larceny touches the honest man, or the law of murder touches him whose hands are stainless of human blood. The thief hates the law of larceny, the murderer the law of homicide. They, too, can truthfully urge the cost of the execution of these laws; both are expensive and onerous to the taxpayer. But I have never known such arguments seriously entertained as a reason for their repeal. The law is without terror save to wrong-doers. The presence of officers of the law only deters criminals from the commission of crime. They are no restraint upon the honest man.

You can form no system of laws which will not be open to some criticism and abuse. These prove nothing against the importance and necessity of their maintenance. If any better method can be offered for preserving the ballot-box in its purity, I will cordially accept it and labor for its passage, but until such better method is proposed we should stand by existing statutes.

"We can not afford to break down a single safeguard which has been thrown around the ballot-box. Every guarantee must be kept and maintained. Fair-minded people everywhere are interested in honest elections. It is not a partizan measure; it falls alike upon all political parties. The law recognizes no political creed, and those who execute it should carefully obey its letter and spirit. It protects Democrats and Republicans and men of all parties alike.

"This House, not content with prohibiting the use of soldiers to keep the peace at the polls, forbidding their employment by the President in any emergency, however grave, now seeks to remove every remaining safeguard to a fair and honest election. The better sentiment of the country, North and South, will not submit to such unbridled license upon the ballot-box. Mr. Chairman, what will the end be? By an amendment to an army appropriation bill which was not connected with the subject matter thereof, peace at the polls can no longer be maintained by the Chief Executive, no matter how grave the emergency nor how pressing the necessity. Tumult and riot may hold high carnival at a Federal polling place, and the Federal arm is powerless to restrain it. This restriction of Federal power, this paralyzation of executive authority, ought to have satisfied the most extreme State rights Democrat; but not so. Having forbidden the use of the executive force to keep the peace at the polls, they now demand that the purity of the ballot and the freedom of the voter shall be subjected to the same lawlessness, with no power in the Government to restrain it.

"Mr. Chairman, my purpose thus far has been to present this law, the repeal of which is demanded, upon its merits wholly. The proposition, however, of the Democratic side of the House is to offer this amendment, not to the sober, independent judgment of the House and the co-ordinate branches of the Government, but to rush it through, right or wrong, justly or unjustly, as a part of a bill making appropriations for the pressing and needful wants of the Government. It is an attempt to do by force what ought to be done, if at all, in the free exercise of the law-making power by each branch of the Government acting in its proper functions under the Constitution. If force and coercion be not intended, then why not introduce and consider this legislation under the rules, with deliberation, and debate upon its own merits, independent and separate from an appropriation bill? This is the ordinary course of legislation, recognized by long practice, founded in wisdom, and never before abandoned for the purposes of coercion. Want of time can not be urged in favor of this course; days of idleness have already been spent sufficient for the purpose. The resort to this method of legislation is a confession of the injustice, wrong, and weakness of the proposed measure, and evinces a determination to accomplish wrongfully that which can not be rightfully accomplished. One of the pretexts urged in favor of placing this amendment upon an appropriation bill is that the law itself was passed by the Republicans in the same way. This impression has become so general throughout the country that it would seem necessary to state the facts in relation to the passage of the Supervisors' law. The law, substantially as it is now in the statutes, was introduced into the House, referred to the Judiciary Committee, considered by that Committee, and reported back to the House by its chairman, where it was discussed, voted upon, and passed entirely independent of any appropriation bill. It took the same course in the Senate. It was not a rider to a bill appropriating money. It is true that the sections extending the supervisors to county districts and restricting their powers in such districts were passed June 10, 1872, upon the Sundry Civil Appropriation Bill.

"The first fruits of their dominion are not assuring to the country, and will not, I am certain, incline the people to clothe them with still greater power. Threatened revolution will not hasten it; extra sessions, useless and expensive, will not accelerate it. Threat and menace, disturbing the business interests of the country, will only retard it. It will come when your party have shown that you deserve it. When you have demonstrated that the financial, industrial, and business interests of the nation are safer and wiser in your hands than in any other, and, more than all, when you have demonstrated that free government will not perish in your keeping, it will come then, and not before. I hope, Mr. Chairman, this amendment will not be insisted upon. It is wrong in itself; it endangers free government. I believe the method proposed under the circumstances I have already designated is revolutionary. There is no necessity for

such haste. The law can have no force and
effect until 1880, except in the State of California. If the amendment must be passed,
let it come in the ordinary course of legislation. There will be ample time at the regular
session next winter, and before any other
Federal elections will be held.

"The country is not asking for it. Business
will suffer and is suffering every day from the
agitation of a continued extra session of Congress. Uncertainty in legislation is a terror
to all business and commercial interests, and
this uncertainty exists and will continue so
long as we remain in session. Let us remove
it. Let us pass the appropriation bills, simple
and pure. Let us keep the Executive Department in motion. Let the courts of the United
States go on and clear up their already over-
crowded dockets. Let the representatives of
the Government abroad, upon whom our commercial relations with other nations so largely
depend, be not crippled. Give the pensioners
of the Government their well-earned and
much-needed pensions. Let the Army be
clothed, provisioned, and paid. Do this,
striking out all political amendments from
the appropriation bills, adjourn speedily, and
give the country that peace and rest which
will be promotive of the public good. When
we have done this we have evidenced the

wisdom of statesmen and the work of patriots. [Great applause on the Republican side.] Let the people then, the final arbiter, the source of all power, decide the issue between us."—*House of Representatives, April 18, 1879.*

CHAPTER IV.

FINANCE.

THE two selections here presented on finance are not voluminous, but they tell the whole story. In the first McKinley arraigns the Democratic financial policy, and in the second states his views concerning silver. No clearer exposition could have been made, or one more consistently Republican.

I. The Purchase of Government Bonds.

"AND I charge here to-day that the President of the United States and his administration are solely responsible for whatever congested condition we have in the Treasury and whatever alarm prevails about the finances of the country. Every dollar of it would have paid a dollar of the Government debts if the Secretary had exercised wisely the discretion given him by law. His way might have been justifiable if there had been no other means of putting the surplus money in circulation. He may lecture that side of the House as much as he will — doubtless they deserve it — but he can not avoid or evade the responsibility that rests on him. What does a man do who has a surplus

balance in the banks and has outstanding
debts bearing interest? He calls in the evidence of those debts and pays them off with
his surplus deposit. That is what a business
man would have done; that is what a business administration would have done; and
we would have had $50,000,000 less of inter-
est-bearing bonds in circulation to-day if the
President had followed the way blazed for
him by the Republican party.

"Well, now, I wonder, Mr. Chairman, if
there was any ulterior motive in piling up
this surplus? I wonder if it was not for the
purpose of creating a condition of things in
the country which would get up a scare and
stampede the country against the protective
system? I wonder if this was not just what
was in the mind of the President: 'I will pile
up this money in the Treasury, $65,000,000
of it, and then I will tell Congress that the
country will be filled with widespread disaster
and financial ruin if it does not reduce the
tariff duties?' If the President thought that
he was going to get up a storm of indignation
and recruit the free-trade army, break down
the American system of protection, and put
the free traders on top, he has probably discovered his blunder by this time; and the
best evidence of it is that he now wants the
very law which he has so long discredited

solemnly re-enacted, as if it were new and
original with him ; and so, having failed, he
comes here through his Secretary of the
Treasury — and I hope, Mr. Chairman, that
the gentleman from Texas will read the letter
of the Secretary upon this subject — he
comes here through his Secretary and asks us
to pass this bill, which is a duplicate of existing law.

II. The Silver Bill.

" *Mr. Speaker:* — It seems to me that the subject now under consideration is grave enough
in every aspect to cause us, even at this last
moment of the discussion, to pause and
thoughtfully consider whether by our votes
here to-day we shall reverse the well-estab-
lished financial policy of the country. From
1793 to 1873 we had the free and unlimited
coinage of silver in the United States, the two
metals fluctuating in value from time to time,
rarely if ever at a parity, sometimes so vary-
ing and unequal that the President of the
United States was compelled to suspend the
coinage of the silver dollar — a rule made by
Jefferson in 1805 and followed for thirty years
afterward. What we are considering here
to-day, and what we have been considering
almost without interruption for the last ten
days, has been only the struggle of the cen-

tury which has vexed the statesmen of all
periods of our history, and that struggle has
been to preserve the concurrent circulation of
gold and silver, each on a parity with the
other. And we have never been able to do it
until now. At no time in the history of the
United States have gold and silver so circulated side by side, in equal volume, as gold
and silver have circulated concurrently since
1878.

"I believe, Mr. Speaker, that we should
preserve these two moneys side by side. And
it is because I want to preserve these equal
standards of value that I have opposed and
shall oppose concurrence in the Senate
amendments. I do not want gold at a premium, I do not want silver at a discount, or
vice versa, but I want both metals side by side,
equal in purchasing power and in legal-tender
quality, equal in power to perform the functions of money with which to do the business
and move the commerce of the United States.
To tell me that the free and unlimited coinage
of the world, in the absence of coöperation on
the part of other commercial nations, will not
bring gold to a premium, is to deny all history
and the weight of all financial experience.
The very instant that you have opened up our
mints to the silver bullion of the world inde-
pendently of international action, that very

instant, or in a brief time at best, you have
sent gold to a premium; and when you have
sent gold to a premium, then you have put it
in great measure into disuse, and we are
remitted to the single standard, that of silver
alone; we have deprived ourselves of the
active use of both metals. It is only because
of the safe and conservative financial policy
of the Republican party, aided by the conservative men of both parties, which has more
than once received the approval of the country, that since 1878 by our legislation we have
compelled gold and silver to work together
upon an equality, both employed as safe
means of exchange in the business of our
country. Let the bullion of the world come
into this market from Europe and Asia, and
then, whether gold flows out of this country or
not, it flows out of the channels of business
and the avenues of trade, and we are in
danger of being driven to the use of silver
alone. I oppose the Senate amendments
because I want the use of both silver and
gold. The gentlemen who favor the amendments of the Senate want silver to do the
work alone, to be the sole agency of our
exchanges.

"Those of us who believe in conservative
legislation want to utilize both metals and
make both respond to the wants of trade.

They talk about silver being cheap money. And gentlemen no longer conceal, on that side and on this, that the reason they want silver is because it is cheap. I am not attracted by the word ' cheap,' whether applied to nations or to men, or whether it is applied to money. Whatever dollars we have in this country must be good dollars, as good in the hands of the poor as the rich; equal dollars, equal in inherent merit, equal in purchasing power, whether they be paper dollars, or gold dollars, or silver dollars, or Treasury notes — each convertible into the other and each exchangeable for the other, because each is based upon equal value, and has behind it equal security; good, not by the fiat of law alone, but good because the whole commercial world recognizes its inherent and inextinguishable value. There should be no speculative features in our money, no opportunity for speculation in the exchanges of the people. They must be safe and stable. And I stand here to-day, speaking not for a single section, but for my country and for the whole country. I say that it is for the highest and best interests of all that, whatever money we have, it must be based upon both gold and silver, and represent the best money in the world."— *House of Representatives, June 25, 1890.*

CHAPTER V.

THE INTERESTS OF LABOR.

McKinley belongs to the common people. A son of sturdy, industrious parents of limited means, he has worked his own way over the successive rounds of effort to the eminence he now enjoys. He never forgets those who toil, and with the great American masses, in their aspirations for better things, his heart beats in warmest sympathy.

I. Multum in Parvo.

"WE are a nation of working people. We glory in the fact that in the dignity and elevation of labor we find our greatest distinction among the nations of earth."—*Chicago, July 4, 1895.*

"If I were called upon to say what, in my opinion, constitutes the strength, security, and integrity of our Government, I would say the American home. It lies at the beginning; it is the foundation of a pure national life. The good home makes the good citizen, the good citizen makes wholesome public sentiment, and good government necessarily follows."—*Cincinnati, O., Labor Day, Sept. 1, 1891.*

"When we constitute eight hours a day's work, instead of ten hours, every four days give an additional day's work to some workingman who may not have any employment at all. It is one more day's work, one more day's wages, one more opportunity for work and wages, an increased demand for labor. Therefore, I am in favor of this bill."—*House of Representatives, Fifty-first Congress, August 28, 1890.*

II. The American Workingman.

"The ideals of yesterday are the truths of to-day. What we hope for and aspire to now we will realize in the future if we are prudent and careful. If right is on our side, and we pursue resolute but orderly methods to secure our end, it is sure to come. There is no better way of securing what we want, and what we believe is best for us and those for whom we have a care, than the old way of striving earnestly and honestly for it. The labor of the country constitutes its strength and its wealth, and the better that labor is conditioned, the higher its rewards, the wider its opportunities, and the greater its comforts and refinements, the better will be our civilization, the more sacred will be our homes, the more capable our children, and the nobler will be the destiny which awaits us. We can only walk in the path of right, resolutely insisting on the right, always being sure at the same time that we are right ourselves, and time will bring the victories. To labor is accorded its full share of the advantages of a government like ours. None more than the laborers enjoy the benefits and blessings which our free institutions make. This country differs in many and essential respects from other countries, and, as is often said, it is just this difference which makes us the best of all. It is the difference between our political equality and the caste conditions of other nations which elevates and enlightens the American laborer, and inspires within him a feeling of pride and manhood. It is the difference in recompense received by him for his labor and that received by the foreigner which enables him to acquire for himself and his a cheery home and the comforts of life. It is the difference between our educational facilities and the less liberal opportunities for learning in other lands which vouchsafes to him the priceless privilege of rearing a happy, intelligent, and God - fearing family. The great Matthew Arnold has truly said, ' America holds the future.' It is in commemoration of the achievements of labor in the past that Labor Day was established. It was eminently fitting that the people should turn aside on one day of the year from their usual vocation and rejoice together over the unequaled prosperity that has been vouchsafed to them. The triumphs of American labor can not easily be recited nor its trophies enumerated. But, great as they have been in the past, I am fully convinced that there are richer rewards in store for labor in the future." — *Cincinnati, O., Sept. 1, 1891.*

III.   The Eight-hour Law.

"*Mr. Speaker:* — I am in favor of this bill. It has been said that it is a bill to limit the opportunity of the workingman to gain a livelihood. This is not true ; it will have the opposite effect. So far as the Government of the United States as an employer is concerned, in the limitation for a day's work provided in this bill to eight hours, instead of putting any limitation upon the opportunity of the American freeman to earn a living, it increases and enlarges his opportunity. Eight hours under the laws of the United States constitute a day's work. That law has been on our statute-books for twenty-two years. In all these years it has been 'the word of promise to the ear,' but by the Government of the United States it has been 'broken to the hope.' The Gov-

ernment and its officials should be swift to
execute and enforce its own laws; failure in
this particular is most reprehensible. Now, it
must be remembered that when we constitute
eight hours a day's work, instead of ten hours,
every four days give an additional day's work
to some workingman who may not have any
employment at all. It is one more day's work,
one more day's wages, one more opportunity
for work and wages, an increased demand for
labor. I am in favor of this bill as it is
amended by the motion of the gentleman from
Maryland. It applies now only to the labor
of men's hands. It applies only to their
work. It does not apply to material, it does
not apply to transportation. It only applies
to the actual labor, skilled or unskilled, employed on public works and in the execution
of the contracts of the Government. And
the Government of the United States ought,
finally and in good faith, to set this example
of eight hours as constituting a day's work required of laboring men in the service of the
United States. The tendency of the times the
world over is for shorter hours for labor,
shorter hours in the interest of health, shorter
hours in the interest of humanity, shorter hours
in the interest of the home and the family;
and the United States can do no better service to labor and to its own citizens than to

set the example to States, to corporations and to individuals employing men by declaring that, so far as the Government is concerned, eight hours shall constitute a day's work, and be all that is required of its laboring force. This bill should be passed. My colleague, Mr. Morey, has stated what we owe the family in this connection, and Cardinal Manning, in a recent article, spoke noble words on the general subject when he said :

" ' But if the domestic life of the people be vital above all, if the peace, the purity of homes, the education of children, the duties of wives and mothers, the duties of husbands and of fathers be written in the natural law of mankind, and if these things are sacred, far beyond anything that can be sold in the market, then I say, if the hours of labor resulting from the unregulated sale of a man's strength and skill shall lead to the destruction of domestic life, to the neglect of children, to turning wives and mothers into living machines, and of fathers and husbands into — what shall I say, creatures of burden? — I will not say any other word — who rise up before the sun, and come back when it is set, wearied and able only to take food and lie down to rest, the domestic life of men exists no longer, and we dare not go on in this path.'

" We owe something to the care, the eleva tion, the dignity, and the education of labor. We owe something to the workingmen and the families of the workingmen throughout the United States, who constitute the large body of our population, and this bill is a step in the right direction." — *House of Representatives. August 28, 1890.*

CHAPTER VI.

EDUCATIONAL TOPICS.

ALTHOUGH McKinley's own education was not extensive, no man appreciates better than he the advantages of learning and the delights of culture. The true meaning of these things he rightly estimates. Education is an American hobby. So is it a hobby of McKinley.

I. In a Nut-shell.

"AN open schoolhouse, free to all, evidences the highest type of advanced civilization. It is the gateway to progress, prosperity, and honor — the best security for the liberties and independence of the people. It is better than garrisons and guns, than forts and fleets. An educated people governed by true, moral principles, can never take a backward step, nor be dispossessed of their citizenship or liberties." — *Canal Fulton, O., August 30, 1887.*

II. Our Public Schools.

"One thing essential to 'getting on in the world' is to have a purpose. Life without it will prove a failure, and all your efforts barren of results. Drifting will not do. You must have a port in view, from which storms and tempests, while they may divert your course for the time, can only delay, not defeat, your ultimate landing. Seek the calling to which you seem best adapted, and then do not expect too large results. Every legitimate calling is honorable, if we make it so, and leads to honor. Every young man should not enter what is called the 'learned professions,' for all are not fitted to prosecute them successfully. The avenues to useful employment, just as honorable and lucrative, are open upon every hand. The 'learned professions' are no longer the exclusive stepping-stones to official honor and the State's highest trusts. I would rather be able to shovel sand well than be a blundering doctor, a pettifogging lawyer, or an unsuccessful preacher, whom no congregation would welcome. It is far better to be at the head of any honorable occupation, however lowly, than to be at the foot of the highest, no matter how exalted. Go at that which will secure you the front rank and give you a place in the front row. The rear rank and the back seat are doubtless indispensable in the march of mankind, but let the man occupy them who can do no better.

" Public instruction wields a power vast

and far-reaching in its results. It was true, as the military attaché wrote to his master, the lesser Napoleon, that 'the schoolmaster, not the needle-gun, triumphed at Sadowa. Knowledge, ideas, convictions, guided by a good conscience, win more battles for mankind than bullet or shell. Prussia was regenerated, under the lead of Von Hardenberg and Von Stein, by the system of common-school education. In the United States, education has always been the national instinct; an enlightened citizenship is now, as ever before, the hope of the Republic. Our country owes much, immeasurably more than aught else, to her educational system, and we must appreciate more and more, as her growth continues and her power increases, that the hope of the Republic is in an educated and enlightened citizenship, which fears God and walks uprightly. I congratulate you upon the completion of this imposing structure, and still more upon the grand uses to which it is dedicated." — *Dedication of Public School, Canal Fulton, Ohio, August 30, 1887.* [*Copyright.*]

III.   From the History of Oberlin College.

"In the winter of 1834–'35, Oberlin College was the first to admit colored students.

This was a mighty and majestic step forward, and it was never retraced. It favored, from its beginning, coeducation. It occupied the very outpost of liberty; it has remained always upon the skirmish line. It is said that, in 1840, one of the young students of the university said to Father Keep, 'When will slavery be abolished?' He answered, with the confidence born of his own faith and courage, ' In about twenty years; ' and that which for so long was only hope and prayer became performance and fulfilment almost within the prophecy of the venerable teacher. The institution was dedicated by its founders not only to the most liberal education, which should include both sexes, all classes, and all races, but was consecrated to liberty and equality among men. These great fundamental ideas have never been for a moment lost sight of since. They have been adhered to in trial and triumph. What influence Oberlin College has had upon the Republic and its citizenship and institutions, no man can tell. It hated slavery, and proclaimed it defiantly. No slave was ever returned from its corporation into bondage, and no slave ever came within its gates who was not welcomed and protected. The case of John Price, the colored boy, who was seized by the United States officers and rescued by the citizens of Oberlin, is now almost forgotten history. That was in 1858, and the whole authority of the General Government was enlisted for the return of that boy to slavery, and yet, in less than five years, the spirit of Oberlin spread throughout the North. Then came the proclamation of Abraham Lincoln that made all slaves free, free to go to every corner of the country within the jurisdiction of the flag. They were earnest, God-fearing men who built your great university; built it, not alone for themselves and their immediate descendants, but for posterity.

"The students of Oberlin College were some of the pioneers in the early struggles to make Kansas a free State. They went wherever freedom was assailed; they literally flocked to that Territory which the South had said should be dedicated to slavery. Their teachers and their preachers went forth from your institution to teach the truth and justice of the Declaration of Independence. Your pupils were in every department of the Army. No more patriotic community existed anywhere in the United States than Oberlin. Your first contribution was a company to the old historic Seventh Ohio, which Captain Shurtleff, one of your professors, commanded. You made contributions to other regiments and to other arms of the service, and every

boy or man who went from your institution
understood exactly what he was fighting for.
Every shot he fired was directed by conscience
and for freedom. He fought not only for the
Union as it was, but the Union as it is, with
slavery destroyed and freedom nationalized.
I have read somewhere that my old friend,
Professor Monroe, with whom I served so
many years in Congress, a man of peace and
opposed to contention, really made the first
war speech that was ever made in your village,
and made it in the old First Church, urging
the boys to go forth and fight the battles of
their country, and that it was his earnest appeal that led to the organization of the first
company that went from the walls of your
institution. It was from your institution General Cox, the distinguished soldier and statesman, went forth, who became a Major-General,
and was the first brigade commander under
whom I served. Hosts of others are promi-
nent in business, in education, in the pulpit,
in literature and in science. The old names
should be dear to the alumni and friends of
the institution : Asa Mahan, John Jay Ship-
herd, Stewart, Shepard, Waldo, Dascomb,
Finney, Dr. John Morgan, Rev. Henry and
John P. Cowles, with many others, contem-
poraries and successors. These names should
not only be remembered and honored at your

reunions, but should be dearly cherished by
you and by the friends of freedom everywhere. I want to congratulate you all on
your achievements, and I join with all in
urging that a fund be raised to enable this
distinguished professor to carry on his work.
Do not give up your peculiarities. They are
excellences peculiar to your own institution.
Stick to them!"—*Annual dinner of Cleveland
Alumni, Cleveland, Ohio, March 3, 1892.*
[*Copyright.*]

IV. Education and Citizenship.

" *Mr. President, Members of the Faculty and
Students of the Ohio State University, and Fellow Citizens:* — The Prussian maxim, 'Whatever you would have appear in the life of a
nation, you must put into your schools,' I
would amend: 'What you would have appear
in the life of a nation, you must put into your
homes and schools.' The beginning of education is in the home, and the great advantage
of the American system of instruction is
largely due to the elevated influences of the
happy and prosperous homes of our people.
There is the foundation, and a most important part of education. If the home life be
pure, sincere, and good, the child is usually
well prepared to receive all the advantages

and inspirations of more advanced education. The American home, where honesty, sobriety, and truth preside, and the simple every-day virtues are practised, is the nursery of true education. Out of such homes usually come the men and women who make our citizenship pure and elevating, and the State and nation strong and enduring.

"It is unfortunate that the great National University which Washington so strenuously advocated was not long ago established, with an endowment commensurate with the dignity and importance of our Government, to which all the universities of all the States would be auxiliary institutions and tributary in the same degree that our public schools are becoming more and more training-schools for the State universities. To my mind the need of such a university is as essential to-day for the welfare of the Republic as the most enlightened and progressive nation of the world as it was in the days of our first greatest President. His great character and broad comprehension not only dominated the age in which he lived, but his advice may yet be followed to the great advantage of the youth of this and future ages.

"In the limitations of an address of this character, it is impossible to do more than allude to the great work of the States of the

Union, in their independent relations, in behalf of education. It has surpassed even the high standard of the nation. Two items may be given in illustration: The total expenditures of the country in support of the common schools in 1870 were $63,300,000; in 1880, $78,100,000; and in 1890, $140,370,000, an average increase of nearly $4,000,000 per annum. The value of school property has also greatly increased. In 1870 it was $130,380,000; in 1880, $209,571,000; and in 1890, $342,876,000, an average increase per year of $10,000,000 for the whole period.

"In addition to this great outlay by the nation and the States, America has just reason to be proud of the private benefactions which her philanthropic citizens are constantly making to her colleges and universities. In the founding of public libraries and in aid of the higher schools from 1871 to 1891 the amount of these gifts exceeded $80,000,000, or more than $4,000,000 a year. I have been pleased to observe that this great University has not been neglected in this regard. The wise beneficence of the late Hon. Henry F. Page, of Circleville, the widow of the late Hon. Henry C. Noble, and, more recently, of the Hon. Emerson McMillin, of Columbus, are examples worthy of emulation by those who have been favored by fortune. Surely accumulated wealth can find no object so deserving and so far-reaching in its benefits.

"But what has been the result of this unparalleled expenditure and munificence? We behold, first, the most satisfactory progress in the public schools, whose enrolment has now reached 13,203,877 pupils, or twenty-three per cent. of our entire population, a greater percentage than that of any other nation in the world. The people were never more willing to pour out their treasure for the support of these schools. The annual expenditure in the United States compared with other countries shows how near they are to the hearts of the people. The expenditure in Italy is $7,000,- 000, or twenty-five cents per capita ; in Austria, $12,000,000, or thirty cents per capita; in Germany, $26,000,000, or fifty cents per capita ; in France, $31,000,000, or eighty cents per capita ; in Great Britain, $48,000,000, or $1.30 per capita ; in the United States, in 1892, $156,000,000, or $2.40 per capita. Our census returns of 1890 show that eighty-seven per cent. of our total population over ten years of age can read and write. 'In the history of the human race,' says Mulhall, the English statistician, 'no nation ever before possessed 41,000,000 instructed citizens.'

"But, Mr. President, we must not forget that the whole aim and object of education is to elevate the standard of citizenship. The uplifting of our schools will undoubtedly result in a higher and better tone in business and professional life. Old methods and standards may be good, but they must advance with the new problems and needs of the age. The collegiate methods of the Eighteenth Century will not suffice for the Twentieth, any more than the packhorse could meet the demands of the great freight traffic of to-day. This age demands an education which, while not depreciating in any degree the inestimable advantages of high intellectual culture, shall best fit the man and woman for his or her calling, whatever it may be. In this the moral element must not be omitted. Character — Christian character — is the foundation upon which we must build if our institutions are to endure. Our obligations for the splendid advantages we enjoy should not rest upon us too lightly. We owe to our country much. We must give in return for these matchless educational opportunities the best results in our lives. We must make our citizenship worthy the great Republic, intelligent, patriotic, and self-sacrificing, or our institutions will fail of their high purpose, and our civilization will inevitably decline. Our hope is in the public schools and in the university. Let us fervently pray that they may always be generously supported, and that those who go out from these halls will be themselves the best witnesses of their force and virtue in popular government."— *Columbus, Ohio, June 12, 1895.*

CHAPTER VII.

MAJOR McKINLEY is a man of deep and sincere religious faith. A member of the Methodist Church, his career has demonstrated that success with one's fellow men is not incompatible with religious profession and an earnest Christian life.

I. To the Epworth League.

"I AM glad and honored to welcome you to the State of Ohio. A return to birthplace is always interesting, and this was the birthplace of the Epworth League. It excites the tenderest emotions and sentiments of the human heart, and recalls the sweetest memories and associations. Such a visit is suggestive of retrospection and introspection, and, if the intervening years have been successful, of congratulation and felicitation. You could have had no better State in which to be born than Ohio, and no better place in Ohio than the city of Cleveland. We are proud of the fact that the Epworth League started here, and rejoice in its marvelous success, and affectionately welcome the daughter to her home and to our hearts. We share in the pride which the Christian world feels over the great achievements already recorded, and of the certain promise of still greater honors yet to be recorded. The purpose of your organization is worthy of the highest commendation. However we may differ in our religious beliefs, your aims command the approval of those who respect good conscience and value good character."—*Cleveland, Ohio, June 30, 1893.*

II. An Auxiliary to Religion.

"*Mr. President, Ladies and Gentlemen:* — I am very glad to join with the citizens of Youngstown in celebrating the completion of this beautiful building, dedicated to the young men for physical, moral, and religious training. I congratulate the young men upon their good fortune and unite with them in gratitude to the generous, public-spirited people through whose efforts this Christian home has been established. It will stand a monument to your city, and an honor to those who have shared in its erection. It will be an auxiliary to all moral and religious effort. It will be the vestibule to the Church, and the gateway to a higher and better Christian life. It will not take the place of the Church, and other agencies for good, but it will supplement and strengthen them all.

" It is a good omen for our civilization and country when these Associations can be successfully planted as a part of the system of permanent education for the improvement and elevation of the masses; it is another step upward and onward to a higher and grander Christian civilization. It is another recognition of the Master who rules over all, a worthy tribute to Him who came on earth to save fallen man and lead him to a higher plane. It is an expression of your faith in an overruling Providence, and strengthens the faith of every believer. You have been made better by the gifts you have bestowed upon this now completed undertaking; you have the approval of not only your own consciences, but you have the gratitude of the present generation, and you will have, in all time to come, the blessings of those who are to be the future beneficiaries of this institution. Respect for true religion and righteous living is on the increase. Men no longer feel constrained to conceal their faith to avoid derision. The religious believer commands and receives the highest consideration at the hands of his neighbors and countrymen, however much they may disagree with him ; and when his life is made to conform to his religious professions, his influence is almost without limitation, wide-spread and far-reaching.

"No man gets on so well in this world as he whose daily walk and conversation are clean and consistent, whose heart is pure and whose life is honorable. A religious spirit helps every man. It is at once a comfort and an inspiration, and makes him stronger, wiser, and better in every relation of life. There is no substitute for it. It may be assailed by its enemies, as it has been, but they offer nothing in its place. It has stood the test of centuries, and has never failed to help and bless mankind. It is stronger to-day than at any previous period of its history, and every event like this you celebrate increases its permanency and power. The world has use for the young man who is well grounded in principle, who has reverence for truth and religion, and courageously follows their teachings. Employment awaits his coming, and honor crowns his path. More than all this, conscious of rectitude, he meets the cares of life with courage; the duties which confront him he discharges with manly honesty. These Associations elevate and purify our citizenship, and establish more firmly the foundations of our free institutions. The men who established this Government had faith in God and sublimely trusted in Him. They besought His counsel and advice in every step of their progress. And so it has been ever since;

American history abounds in instances of this trait of piety, this sincere reliance on a Higher Power in all great trials in our national affairs. Our rulers may not always be observers of the outward forms of religion, but we have never had a President, from Washington to Harrison, who publicly avowed infidelity, or scoffed at the faith of the masses of our people.

" It is told of Lincoln that he once called upon General Sickles, who had just been brought from the field to Washington City, having lost a leg in one of the charges at Gettysburg. His call was one of sympathy, and, after he had inquired into every detail of that great and crucial battle, General Sickles said to him :

" ' Mr. Lincoln, what did you think of Gettysburg ? Were you much concerned about it ? '

" Lincoln replied, ' I thought very little about Gettysburg, and I had no concern about it.'

" The general expressed great surprise, and said that he had understood that the capital was in a great panic as to the outcome, and asked :

" ' Why were you not concerned about the battle of Gettysburg ? '

" ' Well,' replied the simple-minded Lincoln, I will tell you, if you will not tell anybody

about it. Before that battle I went into my
room at the White House, I knelt on my
knees, and I prayed to God as I had never
prayed to Him before, and I told Him if He
would stand by us at Gettysburg I would
stand by Him; and He did, and I shall.
And when I arose from my knees I imagined
I saw a spirit that told me I need not trouble
about Gettysburg.'

"May this institution meet the fullest ex-
pectations of its founders and projectors, and
prove a mighty force in the well-being of the
community! Interested as I am in every
department of work in our State, I can not
avoid especial and peculiar interest in anything which benefits the Mahoning Valley, the
place where I was born, and where I spent my
younger manhood, and around which cling
tender and affectionate memories that can
never be effaced. I am glad to share this
day with you, to participate in these exercises
which open the doors of this building to the
young men of this valley, consecrated to honorable uses, and for their lasting good. I
wish you prosperity in your workshops, love
in your homes, and bid you Godspeed in this
laudable work."—*Dedication of Y. M. C. A.
Building, Youngstown, O., Sept. 6, 1892.*

CHAPTER VIII.

MISCELLANEOUS POLITICAL ADDRESSES.

OF the miscellaneous political addresses from which selections are here gathered, the best thing that can be said to the reader is that they give their own introduction, and from them may be gained a completer knowledge of the versatility of McKinley's genius, and his ready adaptability to the demands of any hour. There is no branch of our public life which his intellect has not illuminated.

I. Civil Service Reform.

"*Mr. Chairman:* — In the single moment that I have, I desire to say that I am opposed to the amendment of the gentleman from Tennessee to strike from this bill the appropriation for the execution of the civil service law. My only regret is that the Committee on Appropriations did not give to the Commission all the appropriation that was asked for the improvement and extension of the system. If the Republican party of this country is pledged to any one thing more than another, it is to the maintenance of the civil service law and its efficient execution; not only that, but to its enlargement and its further application to the public service.

"The law that stands upon our statute-books to-day was put there by Republican votes. It was a Republican measure. Every national platform of the Republican party since its enactment has declared not only in favor of its continuance in full vigor, but in favor of its enlargement so as to apply more generally to the public service. And this, Mr. Chairman, is not alone the declaration and purpose of the Republican party, but it is in accord with its highest and best sentiment — aye, more, it is sustained by the best sentiment of the whole country, Republican and Democratic alike. There is not a man on this floor who does not know that no party in this country, Democratic or Republican, will have the courage to wipe it from the statute-book or amend it save in the direction of its improvement.

"Look at our situation to-day. When the Republican party has full control of all the branches of the Government it is proposed to annul this law of ours by withholding appropriations for its execution, when for four years under a Democratic administration nobody on this side of the House had the temerity to rise in his place and make a motion similar to the one now pending for the nullification of the law. We thought it was good then, good enough for a Democratic administration; and

I say to my Republican associates it is good enough for a Republican administration; it is good and wholesome for the whole country. If the law is not administered in letter and spirit impartially, the President can and will supply the remedy.

"The Republican party must take no step backward. The merit system is here, and it is here to stay; and we may just as well understand and accept it now, and give our attention to correcting the abuses, if any exist, and improving the law wherever it can be done to the advantage of the public service." — *House of Representatives, April 24, 1890.*

II.   Notification Address to Mr. Harrison.

"*President Harrison :* — This Committee, representing every State and Territory in the Union, are here to perform the trust committed to them by the Republican National Convention, which convened at Minneapolis on June 7, 1892, of bringing you official notification of your nomination as the Republican candidate for President of the United States. We need hardly assure you of the pleasure it gives us to convey the message from the Republicans of the country to their chosen leader. Your nomination was but the registering by the Convention of the will of the majority of the Republicans of the United States, and has been received in every quarter with profound satisfaction.

"In 1888 you were nominated after a somewhat prolonged struggle, upon a platform which declared with clearness the purposes and policies of the party, if intrusted with power, and upon that platform you were elected President. You have had the good fortune to witness the execution of most of those purposes and policies during the administration of which you have been the head, and in which you have borne a most conspicuous part. If there has been failure to embody into law any one of those purposes or policies, it has been no fault of yours. Your administration has more than justified your nomination four years ago, and the confidence of the people implied by your election. After one of the most careful, successful, and brilliant administrations in our history, you have received a renomination, an approval of your work, which must bring to you the keenest gratification. To be nominated for a second term upon the merits of his administration is the highest distinction which can come to an American President. The difficult and embarrassing questions which confronted your administration have been met with an ability, with a fidelity to

duty, and with a lofty patriotism which fills
the American heart with glowing pride. Your
domestic policy has been wise, broad, and
statesmanlike; your foreign policy firm, just,
and truly American. These have won the
commendation of the thoughtful and conservative, and the confidence of your countrymen, irrespective of party; and will, we hope
and believe, insure your triumphant election
in November.

"We beg to hand to you the platform of
principles unanimously adopted by the Convention which placed you in nomination. It
is an American document. Protection, which
shall serve the highest interests of American
labor and American development; reciprocity,
which, while seeking the world's markets for
our surplus products, shall not destroy American wages or surrender American markets for
products which can be made at home; honest
money, which shall rightly measure the labor
and exchanges of the people, and cheat
nobody; honest elections, which are the true
foundation of all public authority — these
principles constitute for the most part the
platform, principles to which you have already by word and deed given your earnest
approval, and of which you stand to-day the
exponent and representative. These and
other matters considered in the platform will

command and receive your careful consideration.

"I am bidden by my associates, who come from every section of the nation, to assure you of the cordial and hearty support of a harmonious and united Republican party. In conclusion, we desire to extend to you our personal congratulations, and to express our gratification at the rare honor paid you by a renomination, with a firm faith that the destinies of this great people will be confided to your care and keeping for four years longer." — *Executive Mansion, Washington, June 20, 1892.*

III. Not a Candidate.

"*Mr. President and Gentlemen of the Convention :*—I am here as one of the chosen representatives of my State. I am here by resolution of the Republican State Convention, passed without a single dissenting voice, commanding me to cast my vote for John Sherman for President, and to use every worthy endeavor for his nomination. I accepted the trust because my heart and judgment were in accord with the letter and spirit and purpose of that resolution. It has pleased certain delegates to cast their votes for me for President. I am not insensible to the honor they would do me, but in the presence of the duty resting upon me I can not remain silent with honor.   I can not, consistently with the wish of the State whose credentials I bear, and which has trusted me; I can not with honorable fidelity to John Sherman, who has trusted me in his cause and with his confidence; I can not, consistently with my own views of personal integrity, consent, or seem to consent, to permit my name to be used as a candidate before this Convention.   I would not respect myself if I could find it in my heart to do so, or permit to be done that which could even be ground for any one to suspect that I wavered in my loyalty to Ohio, or my devotion to the chief of her choice and the chief of mine.   I do not request — I demand, that no delegate who would not cast reflection upon me shall cast a ballot for me." — *Republican National Convention, Chicago, Illinois, June 23, 1888.*

IV. Prosperity and Politics.

" It is loudly proclaimed through the Democratic press that prosperity has come.   I sincerely hope that it has.   Whatever prosperity we have has been a long time coming. and after nearly three years of business depression, a ruinous panic and a painful and wide-spread suffering among the people. I pray that we may be at the dawn of better times and of enduring prosperity. I have believed it would come, in some measure, with every successive Republican victory. I have urged for two years past that the election of a Republican Congress would strip the Democratic party of power to further cripple the enterprises of the country, and would be the beginning of a return of confidence, and that general and permanent prosperity could only come when the Democratic party was voted out of power in every branch of the national Government, and the Republican party voted in, pledged to repeal their destructive and un-American legislation, which has so seriously impaired the prosperity of the people and the revenues and credit of the Government."

"It is a most significant fact, however, that the activity in business we have now is chiefly confined to those branches of industry which the Democratic party was forced to leave with some protection, notably, iron and steel. There is no substantial improvement in those branches of domestic industry where the lower duties or no duties on the Democratic tariff have sharpened and increased foreign competition. These industries are still lifeless, and if not lifeless, are unsatisfactory and unprofitable, both to capital and labor.

"There is a studied effort in certain quarters to show that the apparent prosperity throughout the country is the result of Democratic tariff legislation. I do not think that those who assert this, honestly and sincerely believe it. It is worth remembering, and can never be forgotten, that there was no revival of business, no return of confidence or gleam of hope in business circles, until the elections of 1894, which, by unprecedented majorities, gave the popular branch of Congress to the Republican party, and took away from the Democratic party the power to do further harm to the industries of the country and the occupations of the people. This was the aim, meaning, and purpose of that vote. With the near and certain return of the Republican party to full possession of power in the United States, comes naturally and logically increased faith in the country and assurance to business men that, for years to come, they will have rest and relief from Democratic incompetency in the management of the industrial and financial affairs of the Government. Whatever prosperity we are having (and just how much nobody seems to know), and with all hoping for the best, and hoping that it may stay and increase, and yet all breathless with suspense, is in spite of Democratic legislation, and not because of it.

"The Republican party never conceals its purposes. They are an open book to be read by every man. The whole world knows them; it has embodied them in law, and executed them in administration almost uninterruptedly since the 4th of March, 1861. It has bravely met every emergency in all those trying years, and has been adequate to every public obligation and public duty. It is dedicated to the people; it stands for the United States; it believes that this Government should be run by ourselves and for ourselves, its simple code is home and country, its central idea is the well-being of the people and all the people; it has no aim which does not take into account the honor of the Government and the material and intellectual well-being and happiness of the people. We can do no better than to stick to the old party — indeed, we can not do so well as to stick to the old party which guided the Republic for a third of a century in safety and honor; which gave the country adequate revenue, and, while doing that, gave capital profitable investment and labor comfortable wages and steady employment; which guarded every American interest at home and abroad with zealous care; which never lowered the flag of our country, but whose business has ever been to exalt it, and whose principles, the application of which has made us a nation of happy homes, of independent and prosperous freemen." – *Springfield, Ohio, Sept. 10, 1895.*

V. Presidential Candidates.

"Among the distinguished names now mentioned in connection with the Republican nomination for the Presidency, we find an eminent citizen of our own State, whom in the past we have delighted to honor, and whose long and useful public career has made his name and fame nation-wide. Four times elected to the National House of Representatives by his home district, three times chosen to the Senate of the United States, the Chairman of the Finance Committee of that honorable body, closely identified with all the great public measures in the past twenty-five years, and himself the author of much of the wisest legislation of the country within that period; elevated in 1876 to the important position of Secretary of the Treasury, his administration of the finances of the nation has been characterized by the highest skill, and his matchless achievements in that department have commanded the admiration and wonder of the financial world ; to him the nation owes a debt of gratitude which his elevation to the Presidency would fitly recognize, and Ohio would honor herself in honoring John Sherman with a hearty and cordial support at the Chicago Convention.

" But if the choice of the Convention shall fall upon the great soldier of the Republic, the leader of our armies, the ' silent man of the century,' General Ulysses S. Grant ; or upon that preeminent citizen of New England, for years the great leader of the popular branch of Congress, now the peer of the foremost Senator in that body of master statesmen, who has always and everywhere boldly defended Republicanism against the assaults of the Democracy, the peerless debater, the fearless statesman, James G. Blaine — let us unite in pledging Ohio's twenty-two electoral votes to the nominee of that Convention, whoever he may be.

" Nearly twenty years ago the Republican party attained national power in this country, and for the most part has held it without interruption since. Its history records the most stirring events in the nation's life, and there is nothing in its long and eventful career of which any patriot need be ashamed, or which any loyal American citizen would efface. Shall the old party be mustered out of power now? Has it done its work? *Thus far it has, and well.*

"It came into power first to drive oppression out and save liberty from a cruel death. Its work is not yet done. Liberty was but half of the great undertaking; after that, security to our institutions — civil and political equality — must be established firmly and forever. Its mission is, therefore, not ended, and can never end until every freeman is an independent citizen, with every privilege of citizenship guaranteed by the Constitution, and until there shall not be within the boundaries of any section of this great country one foot of ground over which our flag floats and upon which a citizen stands who may not speak and think and vote as he pleases.

"Appreciating, therefore, the overshadowing importance of the issues involved; impressed with the absolute necessity of another Republican triumph; and measuring all the difficulties in our pathway, let us summon the requisite energy and make another grand effort to place in power in this Republic the men and the party by whose fidelity and patriotism its life was preserved. Let this contest end in the supremacy of law and loyalty." — *Republican State Convention, Columbus, O., April 28, 1880.*

VI. On Counting a Quorum.

"Gentlemen on the other side insist upon

what ? That they shall perpetuate a fiction — that is what it is — that they shall perpetuate a fiction because they say it is hoary with age, a fiction that declares that although members are present in their seats they shall be held under a fiction to be constructively absent. That is what they are contending for. We are contending that this shall be a fact and a truth, and that members who sit in their seats in this hall shall be counted as present because they are present. They want our journal to declare a lie; we want the journal to declare the truth. And it is the truth that hurts their position and makes it indefensible." — *House of Representatives, Fifty-first Congress, Jan. 30, 1890.*

CHAPTER IX.

MEMORIAL DAY AND PATRIOTISM.

MAJOR MCKINLEY is at his best in a patriotic address. His own early experience in camp and on the battle-field, showing how highly as a youth he loved the Union, has also enabled him the better to estimate the great work of his comrades-in-arms, by whose heroism and devotion our country was preserved.

I. Gems of Patriotic Expression.

"EVERY anniversary, national or local, properly observed, is a positive good. It emphasizes the ties of home and country. It appeals to our better aspirations and incites us to higher and nobler aims."— *Youngstown, O., Sept. 14, 1887.*

"The admonition of Lincoln — to 'care for him who shall have borne the battle and for his widow and his orphan ' — will never be forgotten or neglected so long as the Republican party holds the reins of power. Full justice will always be done to the soldiers and sailors of the Union." —*At Orrville, O., Aug. 26, 1890.*

"There is not a volunteer soldier before me, there is not a volunteer of the Republic anywhere, who would exchange his honorable record in behalf of freedom and mankind, in behalf of the freest and best government on the face of the earth, for any money consideration. His patriotism is above price. It can not be bought. It is not merchandise for barter. It is not in the market. I thank God there are some things that money can not buy, and patriotism is one of them."—*Canton, O., May 30, 1891.*

II. Memorial Day Address.

"This day has been given to the dead, but its lessons are intended for the living. It has been the occasion for a generous manifestation on the part of the people of their gratitude to the men who saved the country in war. But its true intent will have been lost if it has failed to inspire in all our hearts a deeper sentiment of patriotism and a stronger attachment to those great ideas for which these men gave their lives. It is an impressive fact to contemplate that to-day millions of our fellow citizens from every part of the country have abandoned all thoughts of business, and turned their footsteps to the places where sleep our heroic dead, that they may with loving hands

and grateful hearts pay tender tribute to their
virtues and their valor. This consecration day
is a popular demonstration of affection for the
patriotic dead and bears unmistakable evidence that patriotism in the United States has
not declined or abated.

"There was nothing personally attractive
about any of the features of enlistment in the
War of the Rebellion. It was business of the
most serious sort. Every soldier took a dreadful chance. His offering was nothing short of
his own life-blood if required. These, however, then seemed insignificant in that over-
mastering love of country, in that fervent
patriotism which filled the souls of the boys,
in that high and noble resolve which they all
possessed, that they were to save to themselves, to their families, and their fellow countrymen, the freest and purest government,
and to mankind the largest liberty and the
highest and best civilization in the world.
With that spirit more than two million men
went forth to accept any sacrifice which cruel
war might exact. The extent of that sacrifice
exceeded human expectation, but it was offered,
freely offered, for the country. Can we ever
cease to be debtors to these men? Is there
anything they are not worthy to receive at our
hands? Is there any emolument too great for
them? Is there any benefaction too bounti-

ful? Is there any obligation too lasting? Is
there any honor too distinguished which a
loving people can bestow that they ought not
to receive? What the nation is or may become we owe to them. If there is one of
these fighting patriots sick at heart and dis-
couraged, the cheerful and the strong, who
are the beneficiaries of his valor, should comfort and console him. If there is one who is
sick or suffering from wounds, the best skill
and the most tender nursing should wait upon
and attend him.

  "It is interesting to note the size of our
armies in the several wars in which the
United States has participated. The number
of Colonial troops in the Revolution was
294,791. In the War of 1812 the total number of Americans was 576,622. In the Mexican War the troops engaged for the United
States numbered 112,230. The number of
Union troops engaged in the Rebellion was
2,859,000, or three times the combined force
of the American army in all former wars.
The magnitude of the struggle is also strik-
ingly illustrated by a comparison of casualties.
The casualties in the War of 1812 were 1,877
killed in battle, 3,739 wounded. In the Mexican war, 1,049 were killed, 904 died of
wounds, and 3,420 were wounded. In the
War of the Rebellion 61,362 were killed out-

right, 34,627 died of wounds, and 183,287 died of disease. In other words, our casualties in the Rebellion in killed and those who died of wounds and disease were only 15,000 less in number than the entire army of the United Colonies in the war with Great Britain, and two and one-half times the entire force engaged on the part of the United States in the war with Mexico. But it gives us a truer idea of the dreadful sacrifices of the country to compare our casualties with the casualties of European wars. At the battle of Waterloo there were 80,000 French with 252 guns, and of the Allies, 72,000 troops and 186 guns. The loss of the French was 26,000, estimated, and of the Allies, 23,185. At our battle of Gettysburg, the Union force engaged was 82,000 and 300 guns. The Confederates had 70,000 troops and 250 guns. The loss was 25,203 to the Union forces, and 27,525 to the Confederate forces. Gravelotte was the bloodiest battle of the Franco-Prussian War, and the German loss was in killed, 4,449, and wounded 15,189, out of 146,000 troops engaged. Meade's loss at Gettysburg was greater in numbers while he had only one-half as many men engaged.

"The pension list of the Government tells well the story of the suffering of our great army. On June 30, 1893, pensions were paid to 725,742 invalid soldiers, and to 185,477 widows. In the navy pensions were paid to 16,901 invalid sailors and to 6,697 widows, making a grand total of 934.817 pensioners. Our pension roll on June 30, 1893, contained nearly as many pensioners as the entire muster rolls of the United States in the War of the Revolution, in the War of 1812, and the Mexican War combined. Within 50,000 as many names are now borne on our pension rolls as were contained on the enlistment rolls of all our armies in every war from the Revolution to the Civil War.

" My comrades, this long and highly honorable list is being diminished by death and will rapidly decrease as the years go by. The pension roll has probably now reached its maximum. Hereafter it is likely to recede. Death will stalk through that patriotic list with increased rapidity as age overtakes it, as it is hourly doing, that great army of 1861. The older veterans can not last a great while longer. Exposure has hastened to their door the steps of the pale messenger. God grant that while they are still with us they shall enjoy, without stint or grudge, the bounteous benefactions of the country they served and the tender care and the generous respect of their neighbors and fellow citizens ! 'Dis placed from the pension roll' by death carries

no taint of dishonor, raises no suspicion of
unworthiness.   If the pension roll is diminished, or displacement occurs from other
causes, let it be for reasons just and honorable.   Then the patriotic sentiment of the
country will approve and the soldiers of the
Republic will be quick to applaud.   Let us
care for the needy survivors of that great
struggle in the true spirit of him who promised that the nation would 'care for him who
shall have borne the battle, and for his widow
and his orphans.'

"Sumter and Appomattox!   What a flood
of memories these names excite.   How they
come unbidden to every soldier as he con-
templates the great events of the war.   The
one marked the beginning, the other the close
of the great struggle.   At one the shot was
fired which threatened this Union and the
downfall of liberty.   The other proclaimed
peace and wrote in history that the machina-
tions which inaugurated war to establish a
government with slavery as its corner-stone
had failed.   The one was the commencement
of a struggle which drenched the nation in
blood for four years; the other was its end
and the beginning of a reunited country
which has lasted now for twenty-nine years,
and which, God grant, may last forever and
forever more, blazing the pathway of freedom

to the races of man everywhere, and loved by all the peoples of the world ! The one marked the wild rush of mad passion ; the other was the restoration of the cool judgment, disciplined by the terrible ordeal of four years bloody war. Patriotism, justice, and righteousness triumphed. The Republic which God had ordained withstood the shock of battle, and you and your comrades were the willing instruments in the hands of that Divine power that guides nations which love and serve Him.

"Howells, thirty-two years ago, expressed the simple and sublime faith of the soldier, and the prophecy of the outcome of the war, in words which burn in my soul whenever I pass in review the events of that struggle. He said :

> "'Where are you going, soldiers,
>   With banner, gun, and sword ? '
> 'We 're marching south to Canaan
>   To battle for the Lord!'

"Yes, the Lord took care of us then. Will we heed His decrees and preserve unimpaired what He permitted us to win ? Liberty, my countrymen, is responsibility ; responsibility is duty ; duty is God's order, and when faithfully obeyed will preserve liberty. We need have no fears of the future if we will perform

every obligation of duty and of citizenship.
If we lose the smallest share of our freedom,
we have no one to blame but ourselves. This
country is ours — ours to govern, ours to
guide, ours to enjoy. We are both sovereign
and subject. All are now free, subject hence-
forth to ourselves alone. We pay no homage
to an earthly throne ; only to God we bend the
knee. The soldier did his work and did it
well. The present and the future are with
the citizen, whose judgment in our free country is supreme." — *Music Hall, Canton, Ohio,
May 30, 1894.*

III. The American Volunteer Soldier.

" *Mr. President and Comrades of the Grand
Army of the Republic, and my Fellow Citizens:*
— The Grand Army of the Republic is on duty
to-day. But not in the service of arms. The
storm and siege and bivouac and battle line
have given place to the ministrations of peace
and the manifestations of affectionate regard
for fallen comrades, in which the great body
of the people cheerfully and reverently unite.
The service of the day is more to us — far
more to us — than to those in whose memory
it is performed. It means nothing to the
dead, everything to the living. It reminds us
of what our stricken comrades did and sacri-

ficed and won. It teaches us the awful cost of liberty and the price of national unity, and bids us guard with sacred and sleepless vigilance the great and immortal work which they wrought.

"The annual tribute which this nation brings to its heroic dead is, in part at least, due to American thought and conception, creditable to the living and honorable to the dead. No nation in the world has so honored her heroic dead as ours. The soldiery of no country in the world have been crowned with such immortal meed or received at the hands of the people such substantial evidences of national regard. Other nations have decorated their great captains and have knighted their illustrious commanders. Monuments have been erected to perpetuate their names. Permanent and triumphal arches have been raised to mark their graves. Nothing has been omitted to manifest and make immortal their valorous deeds. But to America is mankind indebted for the loving and touching tribute this day performed, which brings the offerings of affection and tokens of love to the graves of all our soldier dead. We not only honor our great captains and illustrious commanders, the men who led the vast armies to battle, but we shower equal honors in equal measure upon all, irrespective of rank in

battle or condition at home. Our gratitude is
of that grand patriotic character which recognizes no titles, permits no discrimination, sub-
ordinates all distinctions ; and the soldier,
whether of the rank and file, the line or the
staff, who fought and fell for Liberty and
Union — all who fought in the great cause
and have since died, are warmly cherished
in the hearts, and are sacred to the memory of
the people.

" Mr. President, from the very commencement of our Civil War we recognized the
elevated patriotism of the rank and file of the
army and their unselfish consecration to the
country, while subsequent years have only
served to increase our admiration for their
splendid and heroic services. They enlisted
in the army with no expectation of promotion ; not for the paltry pittance of pay; not
for fame or popular applause, for their ser·
vices, however efficient, were not to be her-
alded abroad. They entered the army moved
by the highest and purest motives of patriotism, that no harm might befall the Republic.
While detracting nothing from the fame of
our matchless leaders, we know that, without
that great army of volunteers, the citizen
soldiery, the brilliant achievements of the
war would not have been possible. They, my
fellow citizens, were the great power. They

were the majestic and irresistible force. They
stood behind the strategic commanders, whose
intelligent and individual earnestness, guided
by their genius, gained the imperishable victories of the war. I would not withhold the
most generous eulogy from conspicuous soldiers, living or dead — from the leaders,
Grant, Sherman, Sheridan, Thomas, Meade,
Hancock, McClellan, Hooker, and Logan —
who flame out the very incarnation of sol-
dierly valor and vigor before the eyes of the
American people, and have an exalted rank in
history, and fill a great place in the hearts of
their countrymen. We need not fear, my fellow citizens, that the great captains will be
forgotten.

*　　　*　　　*　　　*　　　*

"My fellow citizens, the rank and file of the
old Regular Army was made of the same
heroic mold as our Volunteer Army. It is a
recorded fact in history, that when treason
swept over this country in 1861 — when distinguished officers, who had been educated at
the public expense, who had taken the oath to
support the Constitution of the United States
and defend this Government against all its
enemies, when they proved recreant to trust
and duty, and enlisted under the banner of
the Confederacy — the rank and file of that
old army stood steadfast to Federal author-

ity, loyal to the Federal Government, and no private soldier followed his old commander into the ranks of the enemy. None were false to conscience or to country. None turned their backs on the old flag.

"The most splendid exhibition of devotion to country, and to the Government, and the flag, was displayed also by our prisoners of war. We had 175,000 soldiers taken prisoners during the Civil War, and when death was stalking within the walls of their prisons, when starvation was almost overcoming their brave hearts, when mind was receding and reason was tottering, liberty was offered to those 175,000 men upon one condition — that they would swear allegiance to the Confederate Government, and enlist in the cause of the Confederacy. What was the answer of our brave but starving comrades? There could be but one answer. They preferred to suffer all and to bear all rather than prove false to the cause they had sworn to defend.

"Now, so far removed from the great war, we are prone to forget its disasters and underestimate its sacrifices. Their magnitude is best appreciated when contrasted with the losses and sacrifices of other armies in other times. There were slain in the late war nearly 6,000 commanding officers and over 90,000 enlisted men, and 207,000 died of disease and from exposure, making a grand total of 303,000 men. In the War of the Revolution between the United States and Great Britain, excluding those captured at Yorktown and Saratoga, the whole number of men killed and wounded and captured of the combined British and American forces was less than 22,000. We witnessed that loss in a single battle in a single day in the great Civil War. From 1775 to 1861, including all the foreign wars in which we were engaged, and all our domestic disturbances, covering a period of nearly twenty-four years, we lost but ten general officers, while in the four and a half years of the late war, we lost one hundred and twenty-five.

" And, my fellow citizens, we not only knew little of the scope and proportions of that great war, or the dreadful sacrifice to be incurred, but as little knew the great results which were to follow. We thought at the beginning, and we thought long after the commencement of the war, that the Union to be saved was the Union as it was. That was our understanding when we enlisted, that it was the Constitution and the Union — the Constitution as it was and the Union as it was — for which we fought, little heeding the teachings of history, that wars and revolutions can not fix in advance the boundaries of their influence or determine the scope of their power. History enforces no sterner lesson. Our own Revolution of 1776 produced results unlooked for by its foremost leaders. Separation was no part of the original purpose. Political alienation was no part of the first plan. Disunion was neither thought of nor accepted. Why, in 1775, on the 5th day of July, in Philadelphia, when the Continental Congress was in session declaring its purposes toward Great Britain, what did it say? After declaring that it would raise armies, it closed that declaration with this significant language:

"'Lest this declaration should disquiet the minds of some of our friends and fellow subjects in other parts of the Empire, we assure them that we do not mean to dissolve the union which has so long and happily subsisted between us.'

"Our fathers said in that same declaration:

"'We have not raised armies with ambitious designs to separate from Great Britain and establish independent States.'

"Those were the views of the fathers. Those were the views entertained by the soldiers and statesmen of colonial days. Why, even the Declaration of Independence, which has sounded the voice of liberty to all mankind, was a shock to some of the colonists.

The cautious and conservative, while believing in its eternal truth, doubted its wisdom and its policy. It was in advance of the thought of the great body of the people. Yet it stirred a feeling for independence, and an aspiration for self-government, which made a republic that has now lived more than a century; and only a few days ago you were permitted to celebrate the centennial inauguration in this city of its first great President. Out of all that came a republic that stands for human rights and human destiny, which to-day represents more than any other government the glorious future of the human race.

"Comrades of the Grand Army of the Republic, those were brave men whose graves we decorated to-day. No less brave were those whose chambers of repose are beneath the scarlet fields in distant States. We may say of all of them as was said of Knights of St. John in the Holy Wars: 'In the forefront of every battle was seen their burnished mail. and in the gloomy rear of every retreat was heard their voice of conscience and of courage.' 'It is not,' said Mr. Lincoln, 'what we say of them, but what they did, which will live.' They have written their own histories, they have builded their own monuments. No poor words of mine can enhance the glory of their deeds, or add a laurel to their fame.

Liberty owes them a debt which centuries of tribute and mountains of granite adorned by the master hands of art can never repay. And so long as liberty lasts and the love of liberty has a place in the hearts of men, they will be safe against the tooth of time and the fate of oblivion.

"The nation is full of the graves of the dead. You have but a small fraction of them here in New York, although you contributed one-tenth of all the dead, one-tenth of all the dying, one-tenth of all the prisoners, one-tenth of all the sacrifices in that great conflict. You have but a small number here; the greater number sleep in distant States, thousands and tens of thousands of them of whom there is no record. We only know that fighting for freedom and union they fell, and that the place where they fell was their sepulchre. The Omniscient One alone knows who they are and whence they came. But when their immortal names are called from their silent muster, when their names are spoken, the answer will come back, as it was the custom for many years in one of the French regiments when the name of De la Tour d'Auvergne was called, the answer came back, 'Died on the field of honor.' America has volumes of muster-rolls containing just such a record.

"Mr. President and comrades of the Grand Army of the Republic, our circle is narrowing with the passing years. Every annual roll-call discloses one and another not present, but accounted for. There is a muster-roll over yonder as well as a muster-roll here. The majority of that vast army are fast joining the old commanders who have preceded them on that other shore.

> "'They are gone who seemed so great —
>   Gone! but nothing can bereave them
> Of the force they made there own
>   Being here; and we believe them
> Something far advanced in state,
>   And that they wear a truer crown
> Than any wreath that man can weave them.
>   Speak no more of their renown,
> And in the vast cathedral leave them.
> God accept them; Christ receive them.'"

—*Metropolitan Opera House, N. Y., May 30, 1889.*

CHAPTER X.

EULOGIES.

McKINLEY'S eulogies on the six heroes, Hayes, Kelley, Garfield, Grant, Logan, and Lincoln, formed a volume in themselves well worth the study of every American youth. Only in part can these masterpieces of oratory be here reproduced. But from these selections the reader will be impressed with their author's judicious temper, his keen insight into human character, and his warm appreciation of the qualities of true nobility. In these orations one may almost see mirrored McKinley's own character and ideals.

I. James A. Garfield.

" *Mr. Speaker:* — Complying with an act of Congress passed July, 1864, inviting each of the States of the Union to present to National Statuary Hall the statues of two of its deceased citizens 'illustrious for their heroic renown, or distinguished by civic or military services' worthy of national commemoration, Ohio brings her first contribution in the marble statue of James Abram Garfield. There were other citizens of Ohio earlier associated with the history and progress of the State and illustrious in the nation's annals who might have been fitly chosen for this exalted honor.

Governors, United States Senators, members
of the supreme judiciary of the nation,
closely identified with the growth and greatness of the State, who fill a large space in
their country's history; soldiers of high
achievement in the earlier and later wars of the
Republic; Cabinet ministers, trusted associates of the martyred Lincoln, who had developed matchless qualities and accomplished
masterly results in the nation's supreme crisis;
but from the roll of illustrious names the
unanimous voice of Ohio called the youngest
and latest of her historic dead, the scholar,
the soldier, the national Representative, the
United States Senator-elect, the President of
the people, the upright citizen, and the designation is everywhere received with approval
and acclaim.

" By the action of the authorities of the
State he loved so well and served so long, and
now, by the action of the national Congress
in which he was so long a conspicuous figure,
he keeps company to-day with 'the immortal
circle' in the old Hall of Representatives,
which he was wont to call the 'Third House,'
where his strong features and majestic form,
represented in marble, will attract the homage
of the present and succeeding generations, as
in life his great character and commanding
qualities earned the admiration of the citizens

of his own State and the nation at large,
while the lessons of his life and the teachings
of his broad mind will be cherished and remembered when marble and statues have
crumbled to decay.

"James A. Garfield was born on the 19th
day of November, 1831, in Orange, Cuyahoga
County, Ohio, and died at Elberon, in the
State of New Jersey, on the 19th day of
September, 1881. His boyhood and youth
differed little from others of his own time.
His parents were very poor. He worked
from an early age, like most boys of that
period. He was neither ashamed nor afraid
of manual labor, and engaged in it resolutely
for the means to maintain and educate himself. He entered Williams College, in the
State of Massachusetts, in 1854, and gradu- .
ated with honor two years later, when he
assumed charge of Hiram College in his own
State.

"In 1859, he was elected to the Senate of
Ohio, being its youngest member. Strong
men were his associates in that body, men
who have since held high stations in the public service. Some of them were his colleagues
here. In this, his first political office, he displayed a high order of ability, and developed
some of the great qualities which afterward
distinguished his illustrious career.

" In August, 1861, he entered the Union Army, and in September following was commissioned Colonel of the Forty-second Ohio Infantry Volunteers. He was promoted successively Brigadier and Major-General of the United States Volunteers, and while yet in the army was elected to Congress, remaining in the field more than a year after his election, and resigning only in time to take his seat in the House, December 7, 1863. His military service secured him his first national prominence. He showed himself competent to command in the field, although without previous training. He could plan battles and fight them successfully. As an officer, he was exceptionally popular, beloved by his men, many of whom were his former students, respected and honored by his superiors in rank, and his martial qualities and gallant behavior were more than once commended in general orders and rewarded by the Government with well-merited promotion.

" He brought to this wide range of subjects vast learning and comprehensive judgment. He enlightened and strengthened every cause he advocated. Great in dealing with them all, dull and commonplace in none, but to me he was the strongest, broadest, and bravest when he spoke for honest money, the fulfilment of the nation's prom-

ises, the resumption of specie payments, and
the maintenance of the public faith. He
contributed his share, in full measure, to
secure national honesty and preserve inviolate
our national honor. None did more, few, if
any, so much, to bring the Government back
to a sound, stable, and constitutional money.
He was a very giant in those memorable
struggles, and it required upon his part the
exercise of the highest courage. A consider-
able element of his party was against him,
notably in his own State and some parts of his
Congressional district. The mad passion of
inflation and irredeemable currency was
sweeping through the West, with the greatest
fury in his own State. He was assailed for
his convictions, and was threatened with
defeat. He was the special target for the
hate and prejudice of those who stood against
the honest fulfilment of national obligations.
In a letter to a friend on New Year's eve,
1867–'68, he wrote :

"'I have just returned from a tedious trip to Ashta-
bula, where I made a two hours' speech upon finance,
and when I came home, came through a storm of
paper-money denunciation in Cleveland, only to find
on my arrival here a sixteen-page letter, full of alarm
and prophecy of my political ruin for my opinions on
the currency.'

" To the same friend he wrote in 1878 :

"'On the whole it is probable I will stand again for the House. I am not sure, however, but the Nineteenth District will go back upon me upon the silver question. If they do, I shall count it an honorable discharge.'

"These and more of the same tenor, which I might produce from his correspondence, show the extreme peril attending his position upon the currency and silver questions, but he never flinched, he never wavered; he faced all the dangers, assumed all the risks, voting and speaking for what he believed would secure the highest good. He stood at the forefront, with the waves of an adverse popular sentiment beating against him, threatening his political ruin, fearlessly contending for sound principles of finance against public clamor and a time-serving policy. To me his greatest effort was made on this floor in the Forty-fifth Congress, from his old seat yonder near the centre aisle. He was at his best. He rose to the highest requirements of the subject and the occasion. His mind and soul were absorbed with his topic. He felt the full responsibility of his position and the necessity of averting a policy (the abandonment of specie resumption) which he believed would be disastrous to the highest interests of the country. Unfriendly criticism seemed only to give him breadth of contemplation and boldness and force of utterance.

"In General Garfield, as in Lincoln and Grant, we find the best representation of the possibilities of American life. Boy and man, he typifies American youth and manhood, and illustrates the beneficence and glory of our free institutions. His early struggles for an education, his self-support, his 'lack of means,' his youthful yearnings, find a prototype in every city, village, and hamlet of the land.

"His broad and benevolent nature made him the friend of all mankind. He loved the young men of the country, and drew them to him by the thoughtful concern with which he regarded them. He was generous in his helpfulness to all, and to his encouragement and words of cheer many are indebted for much of their success in life. In personal character he was clean and without reproach. As a citizen, he loved his country and her institutions, and was proud of her progress and prosperity. As a scholar and a man of letters, he took high rank. As an orator, he was exceptionally strong and gifted. As a soldier, he stood abreast with the bravest and best of the citizen soldiery of the Republic. As a legislator, his most enduring testimonial will be found in the records of Congress and the statutes of his country. As President, he displayed moderation and wisdom, with executive ability, which gave the highest assurances of a most successful and illustrious administration.

" Mr. Speaker, another place of great honor we fill to-day. Nobly and worthily is it filled. Garfield, whose eloquent words I have just pronounced, has joined Winthrop and Adams, and the other illustrious ones, as one of 'the elect of the States,' peopling yonder venerable and beautiful hall. He receives his high credentials from the hands of the State which has withheld from him none of her honors, and history will ratify the choice. We add another to the immortal membership. Another enters 'the sacred circle.' In silent eloquence from the 'American Pantheon' another speaks, whose life-work, with its treasures of wisdom, its wealth of achievement, and its priceless memories, will remain to us and our descendants a precious legacy, forever and forever." — *Accepting the statue of Garfield, presented by the State of Ohio, House of Representatives, Jan. 19, 1886.*

II. Ulysses S. Grant.

"*Mr. President, Citizens of Galena, Ladies and Gentlemen :* — I can not forbear at the outset to express to you the very great honor that I feel in being permitted to share with you, at the city of Galena, in the observance of the seventy-first anniversary of the birth of that great soldier who once belonged to you, but now, as Stanton said of Lincoln, 'belongs to the ages.' No history of the war could be written without mentioning the State of Illinois and city of Galena. They contributed the two most conspicuous names in that great civil conflict, the civil and military rulers— Abraham Lincoln and Ulysses S. Grant. No history of Ulysses S. Grant can be written without there coming unbidden from every lip the name Galena, and no faithful biography of the great soldier will ever omit the name of his cherished friend, General John A. Rawlins, also a resident of your city. You have a proud history; Grant gave his sword and his service to his country at Galena, and gave the country back to the people at Appomattox. He presided over the first Union meeting ever held in Galena, and he presided over the greatest Union meeting ever held beneath the flag at Appomattox. He was little known at the first meeting; the whole world knew him at the last.

"We are not a nation of hero-worshipers. Our popular favorites are soon counted. With more than a hundred years of national life, crowded with great events and marked by mighty struggles, few of the great actors have

more than survived the generation in which
they lived. Nor has the nation or its people
been ungenerous to its great leaders, whether
as statesmen or soldiers. The Republic has
dealt justly, and I believe liberally, with its
public men. Yet less than a score of them
are remembered by the multitude, and the
student of history only can call many of the
most distinguished but now forgotten names.
How few can recall the names of the Presi-
dents of the United States in the order of
their administrations; fewer still can name
the Governors of Illinois, and the United
States Senators who have represented this
State in that great legislative body.

"This distinguished citizen, whose life we
commemorate, and the anniversary of whose
birth we pause to celebrate to-day, was born
at Point Pleasant, Clermont County, Ohio, on
April 27, 1822. His early life was not eventful. It did not differ from that of most of
the boys of his time, and gave no more
promise than that of the multitude of youth
of his age and station, either of the past or
present. Of Scottish descent, he sprang from
humble but industrious parents, and with faith
and courage, with a will and mind for work,
he confronted the problem of life.

"At the age of seventeen he was sent as a
cadet to the West Point Military Academy;

his predecessor having failed to pass the necessary examination, the vacancy was filled by the appointment of young Grant. At the Academy he was marked as a painstaking, studious, plodding, persistent pupil, who neither graduated at the head nor the foot of his class, but stood number twenty-one in a class of thirty-nine. His rank at graduation placed him in the infantry arm of the service, and in 1843 he was commissioned a brevet Second Lieutenant in the Fourth United States Regulars. No qualities of an exceptional nature showed themselves up to this point in the character of the young officer.

"His first actual experience in war was in Mexico. Here he distinguished himself, and was twice mentioned in general orders for his conspicuous gallantry. He was twice brevetted by the President of the United States for heroic conduct at the battles of Monterey, Palo Alto, Resaca de la Palma, Chapultepec and Molino del Rey. After the war with Mexico he was stationed with his regiment on the Northern frontier, and subsequently on the Pacific coast in Oregon and California, in which latter stations he saw much trying service with the Indians. On July 31, 1854, he resigned his commission in the army, after eleven years' service therein — a service creditable to him in every particular, but in no sense so marked as to distinguish him from a score of others of equal rank and opportunity.

"He was successful from the very beginning of his military command. His earliest, like his later blows, were tellingly disastrous to the enemy. First at Paducah, then defeating Polk and Pillow at Belmont; again at Fort Henry, which he captured. Then he determined to destroy Fort Donelson, and with rare coolness and deliberation he settled himself down to the task, which he successfully accomplished on February 16, 1862. After two days of severe battle, 12,000 prisoners and their belongings fell into his hands, and the victory was sweeping and complete. He was immediately commissioned Major-General of Volunteers, in recognition of his brilliant triumph, and at once secured the confidence of the President and trusting faith of the loyal North, while the men at the front turned their eyes hopefully to their coming commander. His famous dispatch to General Buckner, who had proposed commissioners to negotiate for capitulation — 'No terms except an unconditional and immediate surrender can be accepted; I propose to move immediately upon your works' — electrified the country, and sent cheer to every loyal heart at home and to the brave defenders in the field. It sounded

the note of confidence and victory, and gave
to the Union cause and lovers of the Union
new and fervent hope. It breathed conscious
strength, disclosed immeasurable reserve
power, and quickened the whole North to
grander efforts and loftier patriotism for the
preservation of the Union.

"On March 17, 1864, a little more than
three years from his departure from Galena,
where he was drilling your local company as a
simple captain, Grant assumed the control
of all the Federal forces, wherever located,
and in less than fourteen months Lee's army,
the pride and glory of the Confederate
Government, surrendered to the victorious
soldier. It was not a surrender without
resistance — skilful, dogged resistance. It
was secured after many battles and fierce
assaults, accompanied by indescribable toil
and suffering, and the loss of thousands of
precious lives. The battles of the Wilderness,
Spottsylvania, North Anna and Cold Harbor,
and the siege of Petersburg, witnessed the
hardest fighting and the severest sacrifices
of the war, while the loss of brave men in
the trenches was simply appalling. The
historian has wearied in detailing them, and
the painter's hand has palsied with repro-
ducing the scenes of blood and carnage there
enacted. General Grant not only directed

the forces in front of Richmond, but the
entire line of operation of all our armies was
under his skilful hand, and was moved by
his masterful mind. The entire field was
the theatre of his thought, and to his command all moved as a symmetrical whole,
harmonious to one purpose, centering upon
one grand design. In obedience to his
orders, Sherman was marching, fighting, and
winning victories with his splendid army in
Georgia, extending our victorious banners
farther and deeper into the heart of the
Confederacy ; and all the while the immortal
Thomas was engaging the enemy in another
part of the far-stretching field, diverting and
defeating the only army which might successfully impede the triumphant march of Sherman to the sea. Sheridan, of whom General
Grant said the only instruction he ever required was 'to go in,' was going into the
Shenandoah Valley, that disputed field, the
scene of Stonewall Jackson's fame. Here
his dashing army, driving by storm and
strategy the determined forces of Early, sent
them whirling back, stripped of laurels previously won, without either their artillery or
battle-flags. Schofield had done grand work
at Franklin, and later occupied Wilmington
and Goldsboro, on the distant seacoast, with
a view to final connection with Sherman

These movements, and more, absorbed the mind of the great commander.

"The liberal terms given to Lee at Appomattox revealed in the breast of the hard fighter a soft and generous heart. He wanted no vengeance; he had no bitterness in his soul; he had no hates to avenge. He believed in war only as a means of peace. His large, brave, gentle nature made the surrender as easy to his illustrious foe as was possible. He said, with the broadest humanity: 'Take your horses and side-arms, all of your personal property and belongings, and go home, not to be disturbed, not to be punished for treason, not to be outcasts; but go, cultivate the fields whereon you fought and lost. Yield faithful allegiance to the old flag and the restored Union, and obey the laws of peace.' Was ever such magnanimity before shown by victor to vanquished? Here closed the great war, and with it the active military career of the great commander.

"His civil administration covered eight years — two full terms as President of the United States. This new exaltation was not of his own asking. He preferred to remain General of the Army with which he had been so long associated and in which he had acquired his great fame. The country, however, was determined that the successful soldier should be its civil ruler. The loyal people felt that they owed him the highest honors which the nation could bestow, and they called him from the military to the civil head of the Government. His term commenced in March, 1869, and ended in March, 1877. It constituted one of the important periods of our national life. If the period of Washington's administration involved the formation of the Union, that of Grant's was confronted with its reconstruction, after the bitter, relentless, internal struggle to destroy it. It was a most delicate era in which to rule. It would have been difficult, embarrassing and hazardous to any man, no matter how gifted, or what his previous preparation or equipment might have been. Could any one have done better than he? We will not pause to discuss. Different opinions prevail, and on this occasion we do not enter the field of controversy, but, speaking for myself, I believe he was exactly the man for the place, and that he filled to its full measure the trust to which his fellow citizens called him. He committed errors. Who could have escaped them, at such a time and in such a place? He stood in his civil station battling for the legitimate fruits of the war, that they might be firmly secured to the living and to their posterity forever. His arm was never lifted

against the right; his soul abhorred the
wrong.   His veto of the Inflation bill, his
organization of the Geneva Arbitration Commission to settle the claims of the United
States against England, his strong but concili-
atory foreign policy, his constant care to have
no policy against the will of the people, his
enforcement of the Constitution and its
Amendments in every part of the Republic,
his maintenance of the credit of the Government and its good faith at home and abroad,
marked his administration as strong, wise,
and patriotic.   Great and wise as his civil
administration was, however, the achievements which make him 'one of the immortal
few whose names will never die' are found in
his military career.   Carping critics have
sought to mar it, strategists have found flaws
in it, but in the presence of his successive,
uninterrupted, and unrivaled victories, it is the
idlest chatter which none should heed.   He
was always ready to fight.   If beaten to-day,
he resumed battle on the morrow, and his pathway was all along crowned with victories and
surrenders, which silence criticism, and place
him side by side with the mighty soldiers of
the world.

"With no disparagement to others, two
names rise above all the rest in American
history since George Washington — transcend-

ently above them. They are Abraham Lincoln and Ulysses S. Grant. Each will be remembered for what he did and accomplished for his race and for mankind. Lincoln proclaimed liberty to four million slaves, and upon his act invited 'the considerate judgment of mankind and the gracious favor of Almighty God.' He has received the warm approval of the one, and I am sure he is enjoying the generous benediction of the other. His was the greatest, mightiest stroke of the war. Grand on its humanity side, masterly in its military aspect, it has given to his name an imperishable place among men. Grant gave irresistible power and efficacy to the Proclamation of Liberty. The iron shackles which Lincoln declared should be loosed from the limbs and souls of the black slaves, Grant with his matchless army melted and destroyed in the burning glories of the war; and the rebels read the inspired decree in the flashing guns of his artillery, and they knew what Lincoln had decreed Grant would execute.

" He had now filled the full measure of human ambition, and drunk from every fountain of earthly glory. He had commanded mighty legions upon a hundred victorious fields. He had borne great responsibilities and exercised almost limitless power. He had executed

every trust with fidelity, and, in the main,
with consummate skill. He had controlled
the movement of a larger army than had been
commanded by any other soldier, the world
over, since the invention of firearms. He
was made General of the United States Army
by Congress on July 25, 1866 — a rank and
title never given to an American soldier before. He had won the lasting gratitude of
his fellow countrymen, and whenever or wherever he went among them they crowned him
with fresh manifestations of their love and
veneration — and no reverses of fortune, no
errors of judgment, no vexatious and unfortunate business complications ever shook their
trustful confidence. When he sought rest in
other lands, crowned heads stood uncovered
in his presence and laid their trophies at his
feet, while the struggling toiler, striving for a
larger liberty, offered his earnest tribute to
the great warrior who had made liberty universal in the Republic. Everywhere he went
grateful honors greeted him, and he was welcomed as no American had been before. He
girded the globe with his renown as he
journeyed in the pathway of the sun. Nothing of human longing or aspiration remained
unsatiated. He had enjoyed all the honors
which his lavish countrymen could bestow,
and had received the respectful homage of
foreign nations.

" His private life was beautiful in its purity and simplicity. No irreverent oath passed his lips, and his conversation was as chaste and unaffected as that of simple childhood. His relations with his family were tender and affectionate.

" Only a few years ago, in one of his journeys through the South, when he was receiving a great ovation, some colored men crowded his hotel to look into the face and to grasp the hand of their great deliverer. To this intrusion objection was made, and the colored men were about to be ejected, when the General appeared, and in his quiet way, full of earnest feeling, said : ' Where I am they shall come also.' He believed in the brotherhood of man — in the political equality of all men — he had secured that with his sword, and was prompt to recognize it in all places and everywhere.

" But, my friends, Death had marked him for a victim. He fought Death with his iron will and his old-time courage, but at last yielded, the first and only time the great soldier was ever vanquished. He had routed every other foe, he had triumphed over every other enemy, but this last one conquered him, as in the end he conquers all. He, however, stayed his fatal hand long enough to permit Grant to finish the last great work of his life

— to write the history he had made. True, that history had been already written — written in blood, in the agony of the dying and in the tears of the suffering nation ; written in the hearts of her patriotic people. The ready pens of others had told more than a thousand times the matchless story; the artist had, a hundred times, placed upon canvas the soul-stirring scenes in which Grant was the central figure; the sculptor had cut its every phase in enduring marble, yet a kind Providence mercifully spared him a few months longer, that he who had seen it and directed it should sum up the great work wrought by the grand army of the Republic under his magic guidance. He was not an old man when he died ; but, after all, what a completed life was his !

"Mighty events and mightier achievements were never crowded into a single life before, and he lived to place them in enduring form, to be read by the millions living and the millions yet unborn. Then laying down his pen, he bowed resignedly before the Angel of Death, saying: 'If it is God's providence that I shall go now, I am ready to obey His will without a murmur.' Great in life, majestic in death ! He needs no monument to perpetuate his fame ; it will live and glow with increased lustre so long as liberty lasts and the love of liberty has a place in the hearts of men. Every soldiers' monument throughout the North, now standing or hereafter to be erected, will record his worth and work as well as those of the brave men who fought by his side. His most lasting memorial will be the work he did, his most enduring monument the Union which he and his heroic associates saved, and the priceless liberty they secured.

" Surrounded by a devoted family, with a mind serene and a heart resigned, he passed over to join his fallen comrades beyond the river, on another field of glory. Above him in his chamber of sickness and death hung the portraits of Washington and Lincoln, whose disembodied spirits in the Eternal City were watching and waiting for him who was to complete the immortal trio of America's first and best loved; and as the earthly scenes receded from his view, and the celestial appeared, I can imagine those were the first to greet his sight and bid him welcome.

" We are not a nation of hero-worshipers. We are a nation of generous freemen. We bow in affectionate reverence and with most grateful hearts to these immortal names, Washington, Lincoln, and Grant, and will guard with sleepless vigilance their mighty work and cherish their memories evermore.

"'They were the lustre lights of their day,
The . . . giants
Who clave the darkness asunder
And beaconed us where we are.'"

Galena, Ill., April 27, 1893, Grant's Birth-day.

III.   John A. Logan.

"*Mr. Speaker:* — A great citizen who filled high public stations for more than a quarter of a century has passed away, and the House of Representatives turns aside from its usual public duties that it may place in its permanent and official record a tribute to his memory, and manifest in some degree its appreciation of his lofty character and illustrious services.   General Logan was a conspicuous figure in war, and scarcely less conspicuous in peace.   Whether on the field of arms or in the forum where ideas clash, General Logan was ever at the front.

"Mr. Speaker, he was a leader of men, having convictions, with the courage to utter and enforce them in any place and to defend them against any adversary.   He was never long in the rear among the followers.   Starting there, his resolute and resistless spirit soon impressed itself upon his fellows, and he was quickly advanced to his true and

rightful rank of leadership. Without the aid
of fortune, without the aid of influential
friends, he won his successive stations of
honor by the force of his own integrity and
industry, his own high character and indomi-
table will. And it may be said of him that he
justly represents one of the best types of
American manhood, and illustrates in his life
the outcome and the possibilities of the
American youth under the generous influences of our free institutions.

" Participating in two wars, the records of
both attest his courage and devotion, his valor,
and his sacrifices for the country which he
loved so well, and to which he more than
once dedicated everything he possessed, even
life itself. Reared a Democrat, he turned
away from many of the old party leaders when
the trying crisis came which was to determine
whether the Union was to be saved or to be
severed. He joined his old friend and party
leader, Stephen A. Douglas, with all the ardor
of his strong nature, and the safety and preservation of the Union became the overshadowing and absorbing purpose of his life. His
creed was his country. Patriotism was the
sole plank in his platform. Everything must
yield to this sentiment; every other consideration was subordinate to it; and so he threw
the whole force of his great character at the

very outset into the struggle for national life.
He resigned his seat in Congress to raise a
regiment, and it is a noteworthy fact that in
the Congressional district which he represented more soldiers were sent to the front
according to its population than in any other
Congressional district in the United States.
It is a further significant fact, that, in 1860,
when he ran for Congress as a Democratic
candidate, in what was known as the old Ninth
Congressional District, he received a majority
of over 13,000; and six years afterward, when
at the conclusion of the war he ran as a candidate of the Republican party in the State of
Illinois as Representative to Congress at
large, the same old Ninth District, that had
given him a Democratic majority of 13,000 in
1860, gave him a Republican majority of over
3,000 in 1866. Whatever else these facts
may teach, Mr. Speaker, they clearly show
one thing   that John A. Logan's old constit-
uency approved of his course, was proud of
his illustrious services, and followed the flag
which he bore, which was the Flag of the
Stars.

"His service in this House and in the
Senate, almost uninterruptedly, since 1867,
was marked by great industry, by rugged
honesty, by devotion to the interests of the
country, and to the whole country, to the

rights of the citizen, and especially by a
devotion to the interests of his late comrades-
in-arms. He was a strong and forcible debater. He was a most thorough master of
the subjects he discussed, and an intense
believer in the policy and principles he advocated. In popular discussion upon the hust-
ings he had no superiors, and but few equals.
He seized the hearts and the consciences of
men, and moved great multitudes with that
fury of enthusiasm with which he moved his
soldiers in the field.

"Mr. Speaker, it is high tribute to any
man, it is high tribute to John A. Logan, to
say that, in the House of Representatives,
where sat Thaddeus Stevens and Robert C.
Schenck, James G. Blaine and James A.
Garfield, Henry Winter Davis and William D.
Kelley, he stood equal in favor and in power
in party control. And it is equally high
tribute to him to say that in the Senate of
the United States, where sat Charles Sum-
ner and Oliver P. Morton, Hannibal Hamlin
and Zachariah Chandler, John Sherman and
George F. Edmunds, Roscoe Conkling and
Justin S. Morrill, he fairly divided with them
the power and responsibility of Republican
leadership. No higher eulogy can be given
to any man, no more honorable distinction
could be coveted. He lived during a period

of very great activities and forces, and he
impressed himself upon his age and time.
To me the dominant and controlling force in
his life was his intense patriotism.

"It stamped all his acts and utterances,
and was the chief inspiration of the great
work he wrought. His book, recently published, is a masterly appeal to the patriotism
of the people. His death, so sudden and
unlooked for, was a shock to his countrymen,
and caused universal sorrow among all classes
in every part of the Union. No class so deeply
mourned his taking away as the great volunteer army and their surviving families and
friends. They were closely related to him.
They regarded him as their never-failing
friend. He had been first Commander-in-
Chief of the Grand Army of the Republic,
and to him this mighty soldier organization,
numbering more than four hundred thousand,
was indebted for much of its efficiency in the
field of charity. He was the idol of the army
in which he served — the ideal citizen volunteer of the Republic, the pride of all the
armies, and affectionately beloved by all who
loved the Union.

"Honored and respected by his commanders,
held in affectionate regard by the rank and
file, who found in him a heroic leader and
devoted friend, he advocated the most gener-

ous bounties and pensions, and much of this
character of legislation was constructed by
his hand. So in sympathy was he with the
brave men who risked all for country, that he
demanded for them the most generous treat-
ment. I heard him declare last summer, to
an audience of ten thousand people, gathered
from all sections of the country, at the annual
encampment of the Grand Army of the
Republic at San Francisco, that he believed
that the Government should grant from its
overflowing Treasury and boundless resources
a pension to every Union soldier who was
incapable of taking care of himself, asserting
with all the fervor of his patriotic soul that
the Government was unworthy of itself and
of the blood and treasure it cost if it would
suffer any of its defenders to become inmates
of the poorhouses of the land, or be the
objects of private charity.

"Mr. Speaker, the old soldiers will miss
him. The old oak around which their hearts
were entwined, to which their hopes clung,
has fallen. The old veterans have lost their
steady friend. The Congress of the United
States has lost one of its ablest counselors,
the Republican party one of its confessed
leaders, the country one of its noble
defenders." — *House of Representatives, Feb.
10, 1867.*

IV. Abraham Lincoln.

"A noble manhood, nobly consecrated to man, never dies. The martyr of liberty, the emancipator of a race, the savior of the only free government among men, may be buried from human sight, but his deeds will live in human gratitude forever.

"The story of his simple life is the story of the plain, honest, manly citizen, true patriot and profound statesman who, believing with all the strength of his mighty soul in the institutions of his country, won, because of them, the highest place in its Government — then fell a sacrifice to the Union he held so dear, and which Providence spared his life long enough to save. We meet to-night to do honor to one whose achievements have heightened human aspirations and broadened the field of opportunity to the races of men. While the party with which we stand, and for which we stood, can justly claim him, and without dispute can boast the distinction of being the first to honor and trust him, his fame has leaped the bounds of party and country, and now belongs to mankind and the ages.

"Lincoln had sublime faith in the people. He walked with and among them. He recognized the importance and power of an

enlightened public sentiment and was guided
by it. Even amid the vicissitudes of war he
concealed little from public review and inspec-
tion. In all he did he invited rather than
evaded examination and criticism. He submitted his plans and purposes, as far as
practicable, to public consideration with perfect frankness and sincerity. There was such
homely simplicity in his character that it
could not be hedged in by the pomp of place,
nor the ceremonials of high official station.
He was so accessible to the public that he
seemed to take the people into his confidence.
Here, perhaps, was one secret of his power.
The people never lost their confidence in
him, however much they unconsciously added
to his personal discomfort and trials.

"The greatest names in American history
are Washington and Lincoln. One is forever
associated with the independence of the States
and formation of the Federal Union ; the
other with universal freedom and the preservation of the Union. Washington enforced
the Declaration of Independence as against
England ; Lincoln proclaimed its fulfilment
not only to a down-trodden race in America,
but to all people for all time who may seek
the protection of our flag. These illustrious
men achieved grander results for mankind
within a single century, from 1775 to 1865,

than any other men ever accomplished in all
the years since first the flight of time began.
Washington engaged in no ordinary revolution; with him it was not who should rule,
but what should rule. He drew his sword
not for a change of rulers upon an established throne, but to establish a new government which should acknowledge no throne
but the tribune of the people. Lincoln accepted war to save the Union, the safeguard
of our liberties, and reestablish it on 'inde-
structible foundations' as forever 'one and
indivisible.' To quote his own grand words :
Now we are contending 'that this nation.
under God, shall have a new birth of freedom,
and that government of the people, by the
people, for the people, shall not perish from
the earth.'

"Lincoln was a man of moderation. He
was neither an autocrat nor a tyrant. If he
moved slowly sometimes, it was because it
was better to move slowly and he was only
waiting for his reserves to come up. Possessing almost unlimited power, he yet carried
himself like one of the humblest of men. He
weighed every subject. He considered and
reflected upon every phase of public duty.
He got the average judgment of the plain
people. He had a high sense of justice, a
clear understanding of the rights of others, and

never needlessly inflicted an injury upon any man. He always taught and enforced the doctrine of mercy and charity on every occasion. Even in the excess of rejoicing, he said to a party who came to serenade him a few nights after the Presidential election in November, 1864: 'Now that the election is over, may not all having a common interest reunite in a common effort to save our common country? So long as I have been here I have not willingly planted a thorn in any man's bosom. While I am deeply sensible to the high compliment of a reelection, and duly grateful, as I trust, to Almighty God for having directed my countrymen to a right conclusion, as I think, for their own good, it adds nothing to my satisfaction that any other man may be disappointed or pained by the result.'" — *At Albany, N. Y., Unconditional Republican Club, Feb. 12, 1895.*

CHAPTER XI.

A MUCH larger volume than this could be filled with the occasional addresses of McKinley. It is not claimed for these selections that they do anything more than represent the work of the great statesman and orator, whose real strength the American people are now only beginning to appreciate. These selections will stimulate that wider reading and deeper study of McKinley's thought, to which by intrinsic worth it is so clearly entitled.

I. New England and the Future.

"*Mr. President and Gentlemen of the New England Society of Pennsylvania :* — I make grateful acknowledgment for the invitation which permits me to join in the observance of this interesting anniversary.

"We dwell to-night in history. Reminiscence and retrospect rule the hour and the occasion. We are in spirit with the Pilgrim and the Puritan. This Society is a living tribute to them, and serves to hold in perpetuity, for the present and those who shall come after, the character, courage, and example of those who gave birth to liberty on our soil, and secured political freedom and independence to themselves and their posterity.

" Their descendants, and those not their descendants, in this year 1890, grateful for the inestimable blessings bequeathed to them by the fathers and founders of New England, who two hundred and seventy years ago landed at Plymouth and unfurled the standard of their faith, are meeting to-night in the cities and villages throughout the Republic, to cherish their memories and learn again the lessons of their trials and triumphs. Characterization of the Puritan has been undertaken by author and orator, friendly and otherwise, almost from the time he first set foot on this continent, and I present you that of George William Curtis, as embodying both criticism and eulogy, spoken only as that gifted orator can speak.

" This was his picture of the Puritan :

" ' He was narrow, bigoted, sour, hard, intolerant; but he was the man whom God sifted three kingdoms to find, as the seed grain wherewith to plant a free Republic. He has done more for human liberty than any other man in history.'

" We have a right to take just pride in such an ancestry, to proudly recall the noble men and true women who, braving all dangers and hardships, laid broad and deep the foundations of those institutions that have changed the whole face of the northern hemisphere, and given to the world a civilization without a parallel in recorded history, and to the struggling races of men everywhere assurances of the realization of their best and highest aspirations. We do not pause to discuss their religious forms and beliefs : all will agree that, without loss to religion or piety, a broader and more comprehensive Christian philanthropy now prevails.

" Serious was the character of the Puritans — sober, earnest, stern, full of faith in God and man. They were direct and practical. They indulged little in theory or diplomacy. They dealt with facts and conditions. They were not circuitous or strategic. Their purposes were not veiled, and they struck straight at the mark. The jester and trifler had no place among them. Earnest men and true were required for pioneers in the cause of liberty, and none but such were numbered in that noble band. One hundred and one landed from the *Mayflower*. One-half of their number, or nearly so, died from exposure and hardship during the first year, but those who survived have influenced the character and directed the consciences of the millions who have peopled and who now people this great American commonwealth.

They struck the blow; they endured the privations; they kept the faith, not alone for themselves, but for mankind; they looked forward, and not backward. It was to escape the past and its environments that led them from home, and ties, and kindred. Their opportunity was the new field, their hope and faith, the future, which, under God, they were to make for themselves. For this they suffered; for this they builded, and they builded well and strong.

> "' No lack was in thy primal stock,
>   No weakling founders builded here;
>   These were the men of Plymouth Rock,
>   The Huguenot and the Cavalier.'

" It has been said that New England blood flows through the veins of one-fourth of our entire population. But New England character and New England civilization course through every vein and artery of the Republic; and if the New Englanders are not everywhere found, their light illumines the pathway of our progress, and their aims and ideas permeate and strengthen our whole political structure.

" I have an abiding faith in the ultimate justice of the people. Injustice and wrong can not long triumph in popular government. The future glory of the Republic would seem

to have no bounds set upon it, no limit to its
development or destiny, if all of us practise
the simple code of the fathers, ' Liberty, justice, and equality,' the trinity of their faith and
the corner-stone of our hope. In forgetful-
ness of these fundamental truths lurks the
danger and menace to the future. We need
in this generation that earnest purpose, that
rugged devotion to principle and duty, that
faith in manhood and reliance upon the
Supreme Ruler which marked the early New
England home and character, and that resolute firmness which gave force to their convictions, result to their resolves, and effect to
their laws. This is our anchor of safety.
These annual gatherings of the sons of New
England serve a noble purpose in keeping
alive the spirit of the fathers. God grant that
the fires of liberty which they kindled, and
which have filled the whole world with hope
and light and glory, may never, never be
extinguished!

"I bid you, in the language of the beloved
Whittier —

> "'Hold fast to your Puritan heritage;
> But let the free light of the age,
> Its life, its hope, its sweetness add
> To the sterner faith your fathers had.'

"And, speaking of our country and the

future, I leave you those other words of Whittier :

> "' We give thy natal day to hope,
>   O country of our love and prayer !
>   Thy way is down no fatal slope,
>   But up to freer sun and air.' "

— *New England Dinner, Continental Hotel, Philadelphia, Dec. 22, 1890.*

II. July Fourth at Woodstock.

" *Mr. President, and my Fellow Citizens :* — Since 1870 this spot has witnessed the celebration of the anniversary of our national independence. They have been memorable occasions. It gives me peculiar pleasure to meet the people of New England upon this day, and upon this ground, and especially is it pleasing to me to respond for the first time that I have been able to do so to the many generous invitations that I have received from Mr. Bowen, to whom you and all of us are indebted for this patriotic assemblage. I have liked Henry C. Bowen for a good many things. I have admired him since more than forty years ago, when, in the midst of great political agitation, as a merchant of the city of New York, he said : ' Our goods are for sale, but not our principles.' It was this spirit that guided the

Revolutionary fathers, and that has won for freedom every single victory since.

"Now, what is the meaning of this day and celebration? Simply that what we have achieved must be perpetuated in its strength and purity, not giving up one jot or tittle of the victories won. More we do not ask, less we will not have. There never was a wrong for which there was not a remedy. There never was a crime against the Constitution that there was not a way somewhere and somehow found to prevent or punish; there never was such an abuse that did not suggest a reform that pointed to justice and right-eousness. I am not so much troubled about how the thing is to be done as I am troubled that the living shall do what is right, as the living see the right. The future will take care of itself if we will do right. As Gladstone said in his peroration presenting the remedial legislation of Ireland :

"'Walking in the path of justice we can not err; guided by that light we are safe. Every step we take upon our road brings us nearer to the goal, and every obstacle, though it seem for the moment insurmountable, can only for a little while retard, never defeat, the final triumph.'

"The Fourth of July is memorable among other things because George Washington signed the first great industrial measure on that day. The very first industrial financial measure that was ever passed in the United States was signed by him on the 4th day of July, 1789, and therefore I did not think there was any impropriety in Senator Aldrich talking about the tariff on this day and occasion. It would not be proper for me to make a tariff speech here, although it has been suggested, but I may say with propriety, I am always for the United States. I believe in the American idea of liberty, so eloquently described by Chauncey Depew this morning. I believe in American independence, — not only political independence, but industrial independence as well; and if I were asked to tell in a single sentence what constitutes the strength of the American Republic, I would say it was the American home, and whatever makes the American home the best, the purest, and the most exalted in the world. It is our homes which exalt the country and its citizenship above those of any other land. I have no objection to foreign products, but I do like home products better. I am not against the foreign product, I am in favor of it — for taxation; but I am for the domestic production for consumption.

" In no country is there so much devolving upon the people relating to Government as in ours. Unlike any other nation, here the people rule, and their will is the supreme law. It is sometimes sneeringly said by those who do not like free government, that here we count heads. True, heads are counted, but brains also. And the general sense of sixty-three millions of free people is better and safer than the sense of any favored few, born to nobility and ruling by inheritance. This nation, if it would continue to lead in the race of progress and liberty, must do it through the intelligence and conscience of its people. Every honest and God-fearing man is a mighty factor in the future of the Republic. Educated men, business men, professional men, should be the last to shirk the responsibilities attaching to citizenship in a free government. They should be practical and helpful — mingling with the people — not selfish and exclusive. It is not necessary that every man should enter into politics, or adopt it as a profession, or seek political preferment, but it is the duty of every man to give personal attention to his political duties. They are as sacred and binding as any we have to perform.

"We reach the wider field of politics and shape the national policy through the town meeting and the party caucus. They should neither be despised nor avoided, but made potent in securing the best agents for executing the popular will. The influence which goes forth from the township or precinct meeting is felt in State and national legislation, and is at last embodied in the permanent forms of law and written constitutions. I can not too earnestly invite you to the closest personal attention to party and political caucuses and the primary meetings of your respective parties. They constitute that which goes to make up, at last, the popular will. They lie at the basis of all true reform. It will not do to hold yourself aloof from politics and parties. If the party is wrong, make it better; that's the business of the true partizan and good citizen, for whatever reforms any of us may hope to accomplish must come through united party and political action."— *Woodstock, Conn., July 4, 1891.*

III. Dedication of the Ohio Building.

" *President Peabody, and the Members of the World's Fair Commission of Ohio, and my Fellow Citizens :* — I receive the Ohio building, the keys of which you have just handed me, in behalf of the State, and for the uses of its people. I believe all will agree that your work has been well and faithfully performed, and that the Ohio home you have provided

will be both cheerful and comfortable, as it is
centrally and conveniently located.   It is not
commodious enough to hold all of the Ohio
people who will attend the great exposition,
but they will not all be here at the same time,
and I hope, therefore, that it will be found
adequate for the purposes designed.   The
assemblage of so large a number of Ohio
men and women, with the State officials,
Senators and Representatives in Congress,
the members of the Legislature, a worthy
representation of the Ohio National Guard,
and an ex-President of the United States,
whom we all delight to honor, is of itself an
event of historical interest.   We meet in the
chief city of the great Northwest — a city
which has demonstrated within the past two
days that Congress made no mistake when it
assigned to its enterprising citizens the preparation for the great exhibition which is to
commemorate the discovery of America.   We
are all proud of Chicago and of the great
State of Illinois.

"Ohio, the first-born of the States carved
out of the great Northwest, greets her younger
sister, and congratulates her that within her
jurisdiction the greatest exhibition of the advancement of the arts and manufactures and
of civilization ever known to the world is soon
to be assembled.   In participating in the

dedicatory exercises we not only join in the
world's tribute to the courage and persever-
ance and the inspired purpose of Columbus,
but we do homage to the wonderful products
of man's genius and skill which are soon to
be unfolded before the vision of mankind.
This exposition is not only a thank-offering to
the memory of the discoverer of the New
World; it is in its highest sense the hallelujah
of the universe for the triumph of civil liberty
and Christian civilization. Columbus himself
said he ' only opened the gates;' those who
came after builded, and how well will be
shown in these vast and imposing structures
in 1893. Here in the New World on the North
American continent, in the United States of
America, the Almighty has permitted man the
full development of his God-given rights and
faculties, and opened up to him the widest
possibilities and the attainment of the highest
destiny. Here as nowhere else has been
wrought out the great problem of a free and
self-governed people, and the advantages and
blessings springing therefrom. Ohio has performed no insignificant part in the advanced
position which the country now occupies.
Her people have given their energy and enterprise and their blood without stint for the
accomplishment of what we enjoy to-day.
Columbus, in one of his letters to Isabella,

describing the land and people he discovered, enthusiastically declared :

"'This country excels all others as far as the day surpasses the night in splendor. The natives love their neighbors as themselves, their conversation is the sweetest imaginable, their faces always smiling, and so gentle are they that I swear to your highness there is not a better people in the world.'

"We can almost imagine Columbus had Ohio and her people in mind when he wrote these words. Ohio is the gateway of both the South and West, and she possesses unequaled facilities for both industry and distribution. With such a territory, and the progressive population we possess, under our just laws, Ohio has surpassed the wildest dreams of her founders. It was as William P. Cutler, the son of the founder of the Ohio Company, said, 'Massachusetts and Virginia joined in holy wedlock, and Ohio was the first-born.' We are justly proud of our State. In the Centennial World's Fair in 1876, in the city of Philadelphia, Ohio made suitable demonstrations of her advancement. She will now show the marvelous progress she has made in the succeeding sixteen years. In that period her population has increased over 30 per cent., and to-day our State possesses nearly 4,000,000 citizens, over 74 per cent. of whom were born in the State. What a bond of union among Ohio people, connected by ties of birth ! What a permanent element of citizenship this constitutes; and may it not account for that native pride, that affectionate regard, that tender love for the old State which beats in the heart of every Ohioan?

" It is gratifying to know that the children of Ohio enjoy the very best opportunities for education. It is noteworthy that Ohio employs 25,000 teachers, and that a half million of children daily crowd the doorways of her schoolrooms. Is not this a promising assurance for the future of our great State? I can not refrain from expressing in this presence the pride that I felt at the appearance and bearing of the National Guard of the State, and the other Ohio military companies, which have participated in the events of this week. It is not generally known, but ought to be, that this large body of men came here to participate in the opening of the World's Exposition voluntarily, and with no expense to the State. I know of no better exhibition of interest and loyalty anywhere, and am certain it will not pass unappreciated. Their presence has contributed much to the success of the demonstration, and has filled Ohioans with pride. The Supreme Court, the Legislature of the State, and all the State officials and

members of Congress whose presence we observe to-day, have also given to all Ohioans
special and peculiar pleasure.

"This, however, Mr. President, is but the
beginning of Ohio's part in the Columbian
Exposition. She will be here when the world
assembles at this place — here with the fruits
of her skill, genius, and invention, the products of her fields as well as of her factories,
and I am sure no State in the Union will present a greater variety of productions, or better. It should be the aim of every citizen of
the State to have Ohio appear at her best ;
her rank must be maintained ; she must be
kept to the front. Upon the Commission,
which has thus far done so well, very grave responsibilities still rest, and I confidently trust
to them, with the cooperation of the Legislature, to see that Ohio does not lose, but
gains, in the respect and admiration of all the
people, and makes valuable contributions to
the world's storehouse of learning." — *Chicago,
Ill., Oct. 22, 1892.*

IV. Business Man in Politics.

"Interest in public affairs, national, State
and city, should be ever present and active,
and not abated from one year's end to the
other. No American citizen is too great and

none too humble to be exempt from any civic duty however subordinate. Every public duty is honorable.

"This menace often comes from the busy man or man of business and sometimes from those possessing the most leisure or learning. I have known men engaged in great commercial enterprises to leave home on the eve of an election, and then complain of the result, when their presence and the good influence they might properly have exerted would have secured a different and better result. They run away from one of the most sacred obligations in a government like ours, and confide to those with less interest involved and less responsibility to the community, the duty which should be shared by them. What we need is a revival of the true spirit of popular government, the true American spirit where all — not the few — participate actively in government. We need a new baptism of patriotism, and, suppressing for the time our several religious views upon the subject, I think we will all agree that the baptism should be by immersion. There can not be too much patriotism. It banishes distrust and treason, and anarchy flees before it. It is a sentiment which enriches our individual and national life. It is the firmament of our power, the security of the Republic, the bulwark of our liberties. It makes better citizens, better cities, a better country, and a better civilization.

" The business life of the country is so closely connected with its political life that the one is much influenced by the other. Good politics is good business. Mere partizanship no longer controls the citizen and country. Men who think alike, although heretofore acting jealously apart, are now acting together, and no longer permit former party associations to keep them from cooperating for the public good. They are more and more growing into the habit of doing in politics what they do in business.

" The general situation of the country demands of the business men, as well as the masses of the people, the most serious consideration. We must have less partizanship of a certain kind, more business, and a better national spirit. We need an aggressive partizanship for country. There are some things upon which we are all agreed. We must have enough money to run the Government. We must not have our credit tarnished and our reserve depleted because of pride of opinion, or to carry out some economic theory unsuited to our conditions, citizenship, and civilization. The outflow of gold will not disturb us if the inflow of gold

is large enough.   The outgo is not serious if
the income exceeds it.   False theories should
not be permitted to stand in the way of cold
facts.   The resources which have been developed and the wealth which has been accumulated, in the last third of a century in the
United States, must not be impaired or
diminished or wasted by the application of
theories of the dreamer or doctrinaire.   Business experience is the best lamp to guide us
in the pathway of progress and prosperity."—
*Chamber of Commerce, Rochester, N. Y., Feb.
13, 1895.*

THE END.

www.ingramcontent.com/pod-product-compliance
Lightning Source LLC
Chambersburg PA
CBHW030832270326
41928CB00007B/1006